PENGUIN PLAYS

EDWIN AND OTHER PLAYS

John Mortimer is a playwright, a novelist and a lawyer. During the war he worked with the Crown Film Unit and published a number of novels before turning to the theatre. He has written many film scripts, television and radio plays, including six plays on the life of Shakespeare, the Rumpole plays which won him the British Academy Writer of the Year Award, *Unity*, and the adaptation of Evelyn Waugh's *Brideshead Revisited*. His translations of Feydeau have been performed at the National Theatre. Penguin publish his novels *Rumpole of the Bailey*, *The Trials of Rumpole*, *Rumpole's Return*, *Rumpole for the Defence* and *Rumpole and the Golden Thread* as well as *The First Rumpole Omnibus*, containing *Rumpole of the Bailey*, *The Trials of Rumpole* and *Rumpole's Return*. A volume of John Mortimer's plays containing *A Voyage Round My Father*, *The Dock Brief* and *What Shall We Tell Caroline?*, his acclaimed autobiography, *Clinging to the Wreckage*, which won the 1982 *Yorkshire Post* Book of the Year Award, and *In Character*, a series of interviews with some of the most prominent men and women of our time, are also published in Penguins. He has also introduced a selection of trials from the distinguished Penguin series *Famous Trials*. John Mortimer lives with his wife and young daughter in what was once his father's house in the Chilterns.

EDWIN AND OTHER PLAYS

Edwin
Bermondsey
Marble Arch
The Fear of Heaven
The Prince of Darkness

JOHN MORTIMER

PENGUIN BOOKS

Penguin Books Ltd, Harmondsworth, Middlesex, England
Penguin Books, 625 Madison Avenue, New York, New York 10022, U.S.A.
Penguin Books Australia Ltd, Ringwood, Victoria, Australia
Penguin Books Canada Ltd, 2801 John Street, Markham, Ontario, Canada L3R 1B4
Penguin Books (N.Z.) Ltd, 182–190 Wairau Road, Auckland 10, New Zealand

—

Edwin and *The Prince of Darkness* first published 1984
Copyright © Advanpress Ltd, 1984
Bermondsey and *Marble Arch* first published by Methuen and Co. Ltd 1971
Copyright © Advanpress Ltd, 1971
The Fear of Heaven first published by Samuel French Ltd 1978
Copyright © Advanpress Ltd, 1978

—

All rights whatsoever in these plays are strictly
reserved and application for performance should be made
to the author's agents, Margaret Ramsay Ltd,
14a Godwin's Court, St Martin's Lane, London WC2

Lines from 'Death on Two Legs' in *The Prince of Darkness* © 1975 B. Feldman & Co. Ltd
trading as Trident Music, reproduced by kind permission of EMI Music Publishing Ltd.

—

Made and printed in Great Britain by
Richard Clay (The Chaucer Press) Ltd
Bungay, Suffolk
Filmset in Monophoto Plantin by
Northumberland Press Ltd, Gateshead

CONTENTS

INTRODUCTION

What these plays have in common is that they are short. There are no rules, and a play may be exactly as long as a piece of string. No one complains about a Rembrandt etching because it is not the same size as Frith's 'Derby Day', nor do those who visit the National Gallery to revive their spirits with a look at Cézanne's 'Old Lady' grumble because that experience has occupied them for less than two solid hours. The drama, however, is meant to cover neatly a certain well-defined period of our lives, based, I believe, on something as contemporary as the time it took to digest your dinner at the Trocadero and become hungry enough to face supper at the Savoy.

Films are likewise cursed, and for the worst commercial reasons. Nothing under ninety minutes long can be resold to television. In order to squeeze in a sufficient number of interruptions concerned with floor polish, television sponsors will take no shorter. Even long films with intervals no doubt go on for the sale of ice-creams. Short plays, without intervals, could only deprive the customers of those small hot gin and vermouths it is an impossible anxiety to struggle for in theatre bars. In the future there may be a theatre of continuous short plays which could be seen in the same way as you might drop into an art gallery, stare at one or two pictures that take your eye, and depart as soon as your feet start to ache. At the moment, many plays we are glad to see arrive, linger on for their mandatory two hours, making conversation like those guests who have already rung for a mini-cab which, nerve-rackingly, never seems to turn up.

Whatever their length, I hope at least that each of these productions is a play. How do you distinguish a short play from a revue sketch? I think of a sketch as a caption, a one-line joke. A play, even if it lasts not more than five minutes, should be able to contain at least one life, with a character that can be conceived as stretching backwards and forwards in time, with an existence longer than those moments which actually take place on the stage. A play is a demonstration, in which an audience can recognize something about themselves. As with a picture, this can be achieved by a few lines in the right position.

I have to confess to a low threshold of boredom, and though I have often been with Saint Joan when she picked out the Dauphin, I have not always been among those present when she made her posthumous return to his sleepless bedroom. I have some sympathy with Sir Charles Dilke, who never saw more than one act of any play. He loved the theatre deeply, but enough, he no doubt felt, was as good as a feast. I have even more sympathy with that candid peer who fell asleep during his own maiden speech in the House of Lords. There is something a little desperate about seeing a character who has occupied a year of your life coming through the door at the opening of the third act. 'What, you *again*?' you may be inclined to mutter, gripping the pen to provide him with another, scarcely deserved page of dialogue. In a one-act play the enthusiasm has no time to die. The only rule I have found to have any meaning in writing is to try not to bore yourself.

Edwin was originally written as a radio play, became a television play and is here presented in a stage version.

The Fear of Heaven and *The Prince of Darkness* formed a somewhat metaphysical double bill at the Greenwich Theatre in 1976.

In 1970 I wrote an evening of four half-hour plays which were greatly distinguished by the acting of Glynis Johns, Denholm Elliott, Pauline Collins and Joss Ackland. *Bermondsey* and *Marble Arch* are the short sprints out of that programme which I feel worked best. Needless to say, a half-hour play is exactly twice as hard to do as one which lasts an hour.

John Mortimer, 1984

EDWIN

Edwin was first broadcast by B.B.C. radio on 16 October 1982 as one of its 60th Anniversary Plays. The cast was as follows:

SIR FENNIMORE TRUSCOTT	*Emlyn Williams*
LADY MARGARET TRUSCOTT	*Sylvia Coleridge*
TOM MARJORIEBANKS	*Michael Gough*

Later the play was produced by Anglia Television with the following cast:

SIR FENNIMORE TRUSCOTT	*Alec Guinness*
LADY MARGARET TRUSCOTT	*Renée Asherson*
TOM MARJORIEBANKS	*Paul Rogers*

Scene One: The Truscotts' house, Gallows Corner, before lunch.
Scene Two: After lunch.

SCENE ONE

The scene is the large, moderately well-kept garden of a large Victorian house in the Suffolk countryside. There is a mulberry tree on the lawn under which SIR FENNIMORE TRUSCOTT, *a retired Judge, is sitting in a basket chair and dozing. There are three other similar chairs under the tree, one of which we never see used throughout the play. There is also a garden table. Across the lawn we can see an old, ornate conservatory built on to the house. The conservatory glass is green with moss and algae and opaque, but we can see the shapes of people as they pass through it on their way from the house to the garden.* TRUSCOTT *is in old tweeds, a panama hat is on the ground beside him. He talks to himself as though he is summing up in one of his old cases.*

TRUSCOTT [*to himself*]: I put it to you, Marshbanks, you rogered my wife. The charge is that you, Thomas *Marjorie-banks*, feloniously and unlawfully did roger Lady Margaret Truscott. What day, exactly, what squalid night, or what furtive afternoon? Or was it immediately after breakfast when I had caught the 8.15 up to Temple Station and the Law Courts? Did you dive in here, Marjorie, and take her warm in her housecoat while she was watering in the conservatory? What was your excuse for invading my property? Half a dozen eggs? I remember the nasty habit you had of keeping fowl! That was your war work, wasn't it? Boiling kitchen scraps for a run of bedraggled and malicious birds. Thomas Marjorie-banks, v.c. Violated chickens! A man not to be trusted with anything warm and feathered ... What sort of sentence would that carry, I wonder? Unlawful intercourse with the wife of a High Court Judge, a Red Judge, a Judge of the utmost seniority, what sort of sentence would that attract ...?

MARGARET [calling to him from the half-open conservatory door]: Fen!

TRUSCOTT [*to himself*]: Death is the least sentence I could pass, having given due weight to all mitigating circumstances.

[MARGARET *comes out of the conservatory. She is* TRUS-COTT'*s age but shows every sign of having once been beautiful.*]

MARGARET: What're you doing?

TRUSCOTT: Arriving at some sort of judgement.

MARGARET: Sitting under the old mulberry and dozing. That's what you've been doing. You'll have to bestir yourself soon.

TRUSCOTT: I'm perfectly capable of bestirring myself, thank you.

MARGARET: Edwin'll be here directly. Your son will be here before very long. We're going to lay on a decent spread for Edwin. Have you seen to the wine?

TRUSCOTT: Of course I've seen to the wine. Half a dozen bottles up from the cellar. It's been waiting there for Edwin for most of his life. Patience has made the claret ... something quite remarkable, I fancy ...

[*Pause.* MARGARET *moves away and looks round at the garden.*]

MARGARET: The colchicums are all out. The autumn crocus.

TRUSCOTT: What?

MARGARET: The autumn crocus, Fen. The naked ladies.

TRUSCOTT: Naked ladies! Who calls them that?

MARGARET: Tom does. Tom always calls them 'naked ladies'.

TRUSCOTT [*with contempt*]: Tom would. Tom Marjoriebanks! It all adds up.

MARGARET: Adds up to what?

TRUSCOTT: Small pieces of evidence, all circumstantial. Taken as a whole they provide a pretty formidable case.

MARGARET: No need to think of cases now that you've retired, Fen, dear.

TRUSCOTT: You think I can shrug off the responsibility of judgement with the scarlet and ermine? I'm sitting here in mufti, I know. Under the mulberry. But I still have to reach a *decision*.

MARGARET: We'll soon be having to take in the geraniums.

TRUSCOTT: What have the geraniums got to do with it?

MARGARET: The weather's bright enough now ... but it's decep-tive. I'll soon be taking them in to the conservatory.

TRUSCOTT: Why on earth?

MARGARET: To save them being nipped by an early frost.

TRUSCOTT: Don't mollycoddle them! Anyway, isn't that a job for Cattermole . . .?

MARGARET: Cattermole's got his work cut out . . . He's weeding the cabbages. Anyway, Cattermole's not as young as he used to be.

TRUSCOTT: Don't keep a dog and bark yourself.

MARGARET: The hibiscus came too late! Our soil's not rich enough.

TRUSCOTT: We keep Cattermole as a jobbing gardener and you choose to pot your own geraniums. In my view, you molly-coddle those geraniums. Why can't they stand out in the frost and be nipped like the rest of humanity?

MARGARET: Because they're not at all like the rest of humanity!

TRUSCOTT: Oh, really? What's so different about them, then?

MARGARET [moving towards the conservatory]: They're ger-aniums.

TRUSCOTT: Where are you going?

MARGARET: Just time to water things before I get the lunch laid.

TRUSCOTT: Don't go!

MARGARET: Only into the conservatory.

TRUSCOTT: Isn't that rather asking for trouble?

MARGARET [at the conservatory door]: What did you say?

TRUSCOTT: Typical of a woman. They do rather ask for trouble . . .

MARGARET [opening the conservatory door]: What did you say, Fennimore?

TRUSCOTT: Nothing. I said absolutely nothing.

[MARGARET goes into the conservatory.]

TRUSCOTT [to himself]: Members of the Jury. We now come to the details of this rather sordid story, one that will be painful to you, I have no doubt. It is some considerable time ago now that Lady Margaret Truscott, a woman a good deal younger than she is today, took the unwise step of going, alone and unprotected, into her husband's conservatory for the perfectly proper purpose of watering pot plants. Members of the Jury, you will see that there are two entrances to the conservatory, one leading out to the garden, the other into the hall of the matrimonial home, Gallows Corner near Drackham in the County of Suffolk. The view from outside is somewhat obscured by the greenish haze and deposit of algae upon the glass, and by the extensive fronds of those pampered plants which are apparently too delicate to rough it down the border with the hardy perennials. This makes the conservatory an ideal place for private illegality. An intent observer seated beneath the old mulberry tree on the lawn might have seen, however, through the greenish mist, a second figure invade the glasshouse from the hall entrance and position itself unnaturally close to Lady Truscott. Unfortunately you, Members of the Jury, were not seated beneath that tree on that particular morning. Had you been I do not think you would have been in any doubt as to the marauder's identity. Quite clearly it was none other than the accused, the man Thomas Marjoriebanks!

[*He shuts his eyes. The conservatory door opens and* MARGARET *comes out with a man of the same age,* TOM MARJORIEBANKS, *dressed in a vaguely artistic fashion in a pink shirt, spotted bow tie, old tweed jacket and flannel trousers. He is carrying a tray with a decanter and four sherry glasses.* TOM *is whistling the tune of 'Your Tiny Hand is Frozen' from* La Bohème.]

MARGARET: Wake up, Fen! Tom's here . . . [*To Tom as they walk*] He's dozing again! Dozing under the mulberry tree. Put the sherry down there, Tom, why don't you.

[TOM *stops whistling and puts the tray down on the garden table. He looks at* TRUSCOTT, *who appears to be asleep.* TOM *and* MARGARET *talk quietly, trying not to wake him up.*]

TOM: Time hangs heavy on his hands now, I expect. [*He pours two glasses of sherry.*]

MARGARET: There's so little for a retired judge to do. He's lost without his trials. Of course, he still manages to try things whenever he can. Most of the week he's been trying Haversack for burying his bone in the rosebed.

TOM [*handing a glass of sherry to Margaret*]: What was the verdict?

MARGARET: Not reached. [*She raises her glass to him and drinks.*] Fen likes to drag these things out as long as possible. Oh, and he prepared an indictment against a wasp which kept landing on his toast and marmalade when we had breakfast out here.

TOM: He'd try anything.

> [*He starts to drink.* TRUSCOTT *opens his eyes and speaks loudly.*]

TRUSCOTT: You're right, Marshbanks! Any kind of pest that exceeds its rights.

MARGARET: Surely a wasp has a right to the garden, Fennimore?

TRUSCOTT: Every right includes a duty.

TOM [*pouring a third glass of sherry*]: What's the duty of a wasp?

TRUSCOTT: Not to dabble its feet in my bloody marmalade!

MARGARET: God created wasps, dear. They're entitled to settle. [*She sits in one of the chairs.*]

TRUSCOTT: That's a typical do-gooder's point of view. My wife's a Red, Marshbanks. I hope you appreciate that?

TOM [*handing sherry to Truscott*]: It must be a hard life for you, Fennimore, without any real criminals.

TRUSCOTT: Real criminals? Oh, I can still find plenty of *them*! [*He looks at Tom and drinks.*]

MARGARET [*looking round the garden*]: We're not usually here when the autumn crocus is out. We're usually in Dieppe, the three of us.

TRUSCOTT: I don't like that hotel in Dieppe any more. Not since they put music in the lift.

MARGARET: We could always find another hotel.

TRUSCOTT: Typical Red, my wife. She wants change all the time!

TOM: I missed our holiday this year, all the same. [*He sits and drinks sherry.*]

TRUSCOTT: Can't say I missed seeing you fumble for your francs . . . in slow motion every time 'l'addition' was presented!

TOM: What have you two been doing?

MARGARET: We were arguing about geraniums. Fen thinks I mollycoddle them.

TOM: What do you favour for geraniums, Fennimore? Borstal training? The short, sharp shock?

TRUSCOTT: A little cold weather does no one any harm. I say, Marshbanks, we've not asked you to luncheon, have we?

TOM: Of course you have! Today's the great day, isn't it? The return of the prodigal. What did I smell coming through the house? Fatted calf?

TRUSCOTT [*suspicious*]: Came through the house, did you?

MARGARET: Tom helped me carry out the sherry.

TRUSCOTT: Oh, and what else did he help you do? [*He empties his glass.*]

MARGARET: Nothing else.

TOM: Care for a refill, old fellow . . .? [*He gets up, gets the decanter.*]

TRUSCOTT: *Old*? I like that . . . 'old' coming from *you*!

TOM [*refilling their glasses*]: Here . . . Margaret . . .

MARGARET: Thank you. We're all three old, Fen. No need to rub it in.

TRUSCOTT [*to himself*]: 'Consider my client's age, my Lord. Is he to die in prison?' Why is your client so particular . . . about where he dies?

[TOM *puts down the decanter and raises his glass.*]

TOM: Well. Here's to Edwin!

TRUSCOTT: My boy, Edwin!

TOM: Fatted calf for Edwin. That's what I smelled, coming through the house . . . [*He sits.*]

TRUSCOTT: Not fatted calf. A trifle of roast duck, apple sauce, a loganberry pie swimming in cream. He chose that for his last supper before going back to school one half, I remember. 'Edwin,' I said to the boy, 'if you make such wise decisions throughout your life you will grow to be a great and good man . . .'

TOM: And has he, do you think?

TRUSCOTT: Has he what?

TOM: Grown to be a great and good man.

TRUSCOTT: That remains to be seen.

MARGARET: If Edwin's happy, that's all we care about.

TRUSCOTT: Margaret, being a bloody Red, I mean, would say that!

TOM: Oh, I agree with Maggie.

TRUSCOTT: Maggie . . .?

TOM: Well, with Margaret. What have we to strive for but the greatest happiness of the greatest number?

TRUSCOTT [*with contempt*]: The simple-minded creed of a fellow who makes crockery!

MARGARET: You really cannot describe Tom, whose glazed pottery is shown in *art galleries*, as 'a fellow who makes crockery'.

TRUSCOTT: Crockery or pottery, I don't know what's the difference. Anyway, what's the use of your *artistic* pots, Marshbanks? Anyone ever served up a decent stew in one?

TOM: Anyone ever served up a decent stew in one of your legal opinions?

MARGARET: Oh, well done, Tom! Awfully good shot . . .

TRUSCOTT: It wasn't well done at all! I hope you don't think the judicial function can be compared in any shape or form to spinning a bit of mud around and cooking it into a vague evocation of a peasant chamber pot which can usefully hold dead bullrushes in a Hampstead bed-sitter. Neither has the act of judgement any connection with hand weaving, macramé, petit point or the making of stamped leather covers for the telephone directory.

TOM: At least no one gets sent to prison by a peasant chamber pot.

TRUSCOTT: Exactly! Haven't you noticed, the tide's gone down in this sherry glass? Can I trouble you for another drop of my Amontillado?

MARGARET: Do the honours, Tom.

[TOM *gets up, refills their glasses.*]

MARGARET: I should have liked Edwin to have followed an artistic career. At one time I thought he had a future with the pencil.

TRUSCOTT: He has a far better future than that.

TOM: In the world . . . of business? [*He sits.*]

TRUSCOTT: Margaret can't stand 'business'. She was a pillar of the local Fabians at the time of my boy's birth. You bicycled with them, didn't you, Margaret?

MARGARET: Bicycling was over years ago. We used to go on rambles, though. And summer schools to Dartington Hall ...

TRUSCOTT: A couple of those revolutionary rambles and she thought she'd give birth to Vladimir Ilyich Lenin! Lucky Edwin didn't take after his mother. He found all those Socialists in knickerbockers extremely embarrassing.

MARGARET: I have never seen anybody in knickerbockers! Never in my life.

TRUSCOTT: My boy was always on the side of authority. Edwin was a monitor at his prep school.

MARGARET: I always felt Edwin was too sensitive to be a monitor.

TRUSCOTT: A monitor at Boglands on the Norfolk coast. At 'Boggers' he kept some sort of law and order, in an extremely primitive society. He was a firm but just man, at the age of ten, as I remember it.

MARGARET: He wasn't a monitor at his big school.

TRUSCOTT: His 'big' school? What's this language of the nursery? Lawnhurst. Founded by an Elizabethan clothier. Cold bathed through Victorian England as a harsh nursery for Archbishops and Governors of New South Wales. Edwin's 'big' school. 'Biggies' ... 'Big jobs'.

MARGARET: Edwin was never a monitor at Lawnhurst.

TRUSCOTT: Was he not? I don't entirely remember.

TOM: *I* remember.

TRUSCOTT: What, Marshbanks? What do you remember?

TOM: I remember Edwin wrote to me from Lawnhurst. He said he'd joined the Madrigal Society.

TRUSCOTT [*appalled*]: *Madrigal* Society?

TOM: He said he used to go brass-rubbing in the local churches. On a bicycle. It got him out of the football.

TRUSCOTT: Brass-rubbing! He was having you on, Tom.

TOM: He showed me his rubbings. And some of his water colours were quite decorative. He'd hang them on the walls of his study.

TRUSCOTT: I never saw any such thing ...

TOM: Perhaps he used to take them down when you came to visit, Fennimore ...

TRUSCOTT: All I saw in his study was a photograph of the football team.

TOM: Put up, probably, just to please you.

TRUSCOTT: Why did he write to *you*, anyway?

TOM: What?

TRUSCOTT: Why did he write letters to *you*, from Lawnhurst?

TOM: As a sort of honorary uncle ...

TRUSCOTT: A relation?

TOM: Not really. A family friend.

TRUSCOTT: Friend or relation?

TOM: Just a friend.

TRUSCOTT: No *blood* relation! [*Pause*.] It's wishful thinking, Marshbanks. I don't believe Edwin wrote to you at all. [*Pause*.] You had no issue, did you?

TOM: What?

TRUSCOTT: No fruit of your loins. No part of you whatever, Tom, to thrust forth into the future. You will die and there'll be nothing left of you, except a few impractical china objects and your old tweed jacket swinging on a coat hanger. That is until they pack it up and give it to Oxfam.

TOM: My dear Fennimore. Do *you* claim immortality?

TRUSCOTT: Edwin will carry on a certain tradition. He is carrying on ... certain standards! [*Pause*.] They're keeping him busy out in Canada, apparently. Well, Edwin's not afraid of work. Well, the boy's letters were always scrappy.

TOM: Not at all.

TRUSCOTT: What?

TOM: I said not at all. His letters from school to me were always long.

TRUSCOTT: Long letters to *you*? Oh yes, what about?

TOM: About the leaves falling. About the wind. Breaking into poetry sometimes.

TRUSCOTT: You live in a world of fantasy! [*Pause*.] Any good?

TOM: What?

TRUSCOTT: Edwin's poetry.

TOM: And clouds. I believe it was about clouds. That sort of thing ...

TRUSCOTT: No bloody good then, eh?

MARGARET: Don't you be so sure, Fen.

TRUSCOTT: What?

MARGARET: Don't you be so sure it wasn't good. Edwin had a sensitive ear for verse.

TRUSCOTT: A sensitive ear! I can't say I ever noticed.

[TOM *starts to whistle the* Bohème *aria.*]

TRUSCOTT [*to himself*]: You hear that whistle, Members of the Jury? It may be an important piece of the evidence. [*Aloud*] What are you whistling, Marshbanks, exactly?

MARGARET: He always whistles that.

TRUSCOTT: He always what?

MARGARET: He whistled it, I remember, during air raids.

TRUSCOTT: The war years ...

MARGARET: Such a happy time. The war years. The summers were so marvellous.

TRUSCOTT: And you could have lunch at the Savoy and change left over from a ten-bob note.

MARGARET: And Tom kept chickens. Do you remember, Tom? You used to bring us eggs. [*Pause.*] Tom kept chickens ... and I was pregnant with Edwin.

TRUSCOTT: You were pregnant with our boy, and Tom used to come round whistling.

[TOM *whistles.*]

TRUSCOTT: You used to whistle like a grocer's boy, bringing round eggs. [*Pause.*] Edwin didn't write to you from Canada?

TOM: No. No, in Canada Edwin became strangely silent.

TRUSCOTT: Well, you know what boys are.

MARGARET: Boys?

TRUSCOTT: When they get a bit of independence for the first time. When they go out to the Colonies. Run wild for a few years. Get the edges knocked off them. Well, it's only to be expected.

TOM: You think Edwin's been running wild?

TRUSCOTT: Wouldn't surprise me in the least. I don't mean anything sinister. I don't mean anything seriously immoral. But it wouldn't surprise me if he hadn't been ... well, log-cabinning ... out in the Rockies or somewhere.

MARGARET: His letters to me are all from Global Computers.

TRUSCOTT: Computers? Oh yes. Of course. [*Pause.*] Well, I

expect that's just what he tells his mother. Log-cabinning, I dare say. Something of that nature. [*Pause.*] He's written to you, then?

MARGARET: Written occasionally. [*She stands up.*]

TRUSCOTT: You didn't tell me.

[MARGARET *moves towards the conservatory and the house.*]

MARGARET: I'll go and look at the duck. See if the oven needs turning up.

TRUSCOTT [*calling after her*]: Why didn't you show me the letters, madam?

[MARGARET *goes into the conservatory. We see her shadowy figure disappear behind the glass.*]

TOM: She's gone, Fennimore. Maggie has gone into the house.

TRUSCOTT [*to himself*]: Madam, I demand an answer to my question! The witness has clearly something to hide. You might think that a man, Members of the Jury, would be interested above all things in a letter from his son, his own flesh and blood. [*Pause.*] That is, of course, if he *is* his own flesh and blood . . .

[TOM *whistles.*]

TRUSCOTT [*to himself*]: The presumption of legitimate birth is strong. Nothing is stronger.

[TOM *stops whistling, laughs.*]

TOM: She's marvellous . . . old Maggie.

TRUSCOTT: Marvellous! Is that your view of Margaret?

TOM: I mean. She's a marvellous wife, your Margaret.

TRUSCOTT: *My* Margaret . . . [*Pause.*] Fancy her, don't you? [*To himself*] It is, of course, the vital question.

TOM: Oh, enormously.

TRUSCOTT [*to himself*]: Is the accused suffering from ridiculous over-confidence . . . or is the guilt so great that he sees no alternative to an admission?

TOM [*laughing*]: Of course I fancy her. Always did. Since the first day you brought her here.

TRUSCOTT [*to himself*]: Bringing her here. That was my mistake. To Gallows Corner. Where the next-door neighbour was a lecherous potter. A fellow with nothing better to do than spin shit-coloured crocks for holding spills in front of gas fires in Welwyn Garden City and leer through conservatory windows at the other fellow's wife.

TOM: I remember that first day you brought her here. After your old father died.

TRUSCOTT [*to himself*]: The house was empty. We were picnicking in a dusty kitchen. 'Gallows Corner' seemed an appropriate sort of name, I said, as I'd just been made up to a High Court Judge, a fellow who then had it in his power to order, in extreme cases of course, a good topping.

TOM: She came over to borrow a little milk.

TRUSCOTT: She was always forgetful.

TOM: She wore a blue linen dress, as I remember it. No stockings and plimsolls.

TRUSCOTT: She dressed like a revolutionary. A Judge's wife, wearing plimsolls . . . like a bloody Communist!

TOM: Her red hair was tied back with a ribbon. That was what struck me so forcibly.

TRUSCOTT [*puzzled*]: Red hair?

TOM: Well, surely the colour of her hair is . . .

TRUSCOTT: Grey is what I would say about it. Entirely grey.

TOM: But then . . . then it was red, surely?

TRUSCOTT: I would have described it as auburn. And held back with a tortoiseshell comb. I thought she was a long time borrowing the milk.

TOM: What're you getting at?

TRUSCOTT: I am getting at the heart of this extremely distressing case, aren't I now?

TOM: The heart . . .?

TRUSCOTT [*rising*]: Later, some years later, a person pleading guilty, I left Court early, and, as an unremembered robber started on his ten years of close confinement, I began my sentence of suspicion.

TOM: Sometimes, my dear Fennimore, you talk like a bad detective story.

[TRUSCOTT *turns and looks at the conservatory, takes a step or two towards it.*]

TRUSCOTT: I crossed the lawn and stood facing the conservatory. I heard that damned perky little tune you still indulge in.

TOM [*singing quietly*]:

> '*Che gelida manina,*
> *Se la lasci riscaldar.*
> *Cercar che giova?*
> *Al buio non si trova ...*'

TRUSCOTT: The windows of the conservatory were misted. I saw nothing but shapes.

TOM [*still singing*]:

> '*Ma per fortuna*
> *È una notte di luna,*
> *E qui la luna*
> *L'abbiamo vicina ...*'

TRUSCOTT: What were the two shadows on the greenish glass? A woman and a watering can merely, or two creatures of the opposite sex, unlawfully intermingled? I stood watching a long time. Then I scrunched my foot on the gravel to give you fair warning. [*He moves back towards his chair.*] But when I opened the conservatory door ...

TOM: What did you see?

[TRUSCOTT *sits.*]

TRUSCOTT: My much-troubled wife.

TOM: And ...?

TRUSCOTT: No one else.

TOM: There now! Nothing to worry about.

TRUSCOTT: The bird had flown.

TOM: I was never there.

TRUSCOTT: You'd fled. A very clear indication of guilt.

TOM: If I hadn't been there, I couldn't have fled.

TRUSCOTT: If you hadn't been there you couldn't've been whistling that damned tune!

TOM: Perhaps Maggie whistled it.

TRUSCOTT: My wife would never do such a thing. She's not musical. So far as I know.

TOM: You may not know very far. Your wife is particularly addicted to the operas of Giacomo Puccini.

TRUSCOTT: She never listens to music.

TOM: She never listens, Fen, because she is afraid music would arouse in her romantic longings which you are quite unable to fulfil.

TRUSCOTT: So, do *you* . . .?

TOM: What?

TRUSCOTT: You, Marshbanks, do *you* fulfil them?

TOM: What is the question, exactly?

TRUSCOTT [*to himself*]: The question is, Members of the Jury, have you rogered my wife? [*Aloud*] Have you rogered her?

  [*Pause.*]

TOM: Hadn't you better ask *her* that?

TRUSCOTT: It's not the sort of question one asks a lady, is it?

TOM: Anyway, why bring it up today . . . after all these years?

TRUSCOTT: Isn't this *just* the day to bring it up? Edwin's coming to lunch.

TOM: I see. Oh, I do see. [*Laughs.*] Oh dear . . . Oh deary me. Brass-rubbings! And water colours!

TRUSCOTT [*voice of doom*]: Yes?

TOM: Poor old Fen! You didn't care for the idea of Edwin writing to me about . . . brass-rubbings!

TRUSCOTT: I must confess, I found the evidence disturbing.

TOM: You didn't care for it at all!

TRUSCOTT [*to himself*]: It comes from an unreliable source, that is to say the mouth of the accused, but it is . . . disturbing evidence, all the same.

TOM: What are you afraid of, Fennimore? That I'll take your immortality off you?

TRUSCOTT: What are you talking about?

TOM: Your claim on the years to come. A line of Truscotts, stretching out into the future. Passing judgement. Condemning! Locking people up. Endlessly censorious. Endlessly frightened of what their wives may be getting up to in the conservatory. The Truscotts of Gallows Corner!

TRUSCOTT: Rather a better stock, wouldn't you say, than the Marshbanks of Craft Cottage . . . The potters of Folkweave Farm . . . The old fellows with moist blue eyes and spotted bow ties . . . You know, the ones whose war effort was whistling and keeping chickens. That line is coming to an abrupt end with you, Marshbanks! There will be no fruit of the loins you keep concealed in those filthy old corduroy bags!

TOM: Is that your considered opinion?

TRUSCOTT: What?

TOM: Is that your final judgement on the matter?

TRUSCOTT: Is there anything more you would wish to say?

[*Silence*.]

Mute of malice, are you?

TOM: Is there anything more you would wish me to say?

TRUSCOTT: I'm not fishing for information.

TOM: Oh yes you are! You boast you're such a tough nut to crack but you're frightened. Admit it, Fennimore. Scared to death of what you might discover!

TRUSCOTT: Scared? Scared of what?

TOM: Edwin.

TRUSCOTT: My son ...

TOM: Your son. With artistic leanings. Your son, who wrote to me regularly from Lawnhurst. Your son who's kept quiet all these years, doing what exactly? Throwing pots, perhaps. Using his fingers, light on the clay, a touch like velvet, to achieve a perfect symmetry! Is he really *your* son, do you think?

[*Pause*.]

TRUSCOTT [*furious*]: Have you the slightest evidence to support that monstrous allegation?

TOM: Only the evidence of your eyes. Take a good look at lunch-time, on your idea of the future.

TRUSCOTT: Don't be ridiculous. I've looked at Edwin. I've seen the boy tearing round this very garden. I've bowled leg breaks to him down there on the edge of the paddock. At times ... many times ... I have felt bound to punish him and I must say he has respected me for it. The matter is proved beyond reasonable doubt. All doubt is fanciful. The lad is every inch a Truscott.

TOM: If you think so ...

TRUSCOTT: What?

TOM: I said ...

TRUSCOTT: I heard what you said. I'm not deaf. What sort of answer is that – 'If you think so'?

TOM: It's not meant to be an answer, more a comment.

TRUSCOTT: Not evidence. Pure comment.

TOM: On your enormous complacency.

TRUSCOTT: My ...?

TOM: You're so sure of everything, aren't you, Fennimore? I have sat in this garden now, ever since you moved to Gallows Corner, or at your dinner table or at lunch, and I have been deafened by your appalling lack of doubt on every subject. Capital punishment. Corporal punishment. How to make marmalade. Everything appears perfectly simple to you, doesn't it? God is simply a senior Judge in the Court of Appeal. Death is merely a promotion to immortality. Geraniums are perfectly simple to manage if you don't mollycoddle them. And I ... your next-door neighbour ... I have to stand in, now they've retired you at long, long last, for all those unfortunate criminals you miss so badly. I might refuse to visit you again. I'm tired of standing in the dock at Gallows Corner.

TRUSCOTT: Never visit us ... and not see Margaret?

TOM: And not see either of you. It's been a life's work, keeping you both amused.

TRUSCOTT: Do you suppose I find you *amusing*?

TOM: Oh, of course. My pots. My bow ties. My alleged loose living. They keep you constantly entertained, don't they? And the fact that Maggie and I possibly had ... a relationship ...

TRUSCOTT: Relationship? What sort of mealy-mouthed expression is that? Is that the word nice girls in smocks who hand-paint egg cups use, when they rut? Why don't you say 'roger' like everyone else?

TOM: Because you're the only person I've ever heard say it.

[*Pause.* TRUSCOTT *stands.*]

TRUSCOTT: Have you rogered her? That is the question I have long had before me.

TOM: Well, have you come to a final judgement?

TRUSCOTT: Oh yes.

TOM: And the verdict is 'guilty', I suppose. It usually is.

TRUSCOTT: I have directed myself as to reasonable doubt.

Doubt is, in most cases, a form of cowardice. And now I have the painful duty of passing judgement.

TOM: Why painful? Passing judgement's as natural to you as passing water.

TRUSCOTT: In a shifting world, Marshbanks ... In a bog of unreliable evidence, there is usually one hard fact, one stepping stone of undisputed truth. And that is ... I am Edwin's father!

TOM: The complacency ... of your legal decisions!

TRUSCOTT: Whatever you may or may not have done, and I make no finding as to your activities save that they were furtive, devious and no doubt deeply embarrassing to the lady upon whom you inflicted your attentions – the paternity of Edwin is beyond dispute. How could it be otherwise?

TOM: I thought you had an idea how it might be.

[*Pause, then* TRUSCOTT *sits. He is smiling.*]

TRUSCOTT: The idea is laughable. As you pass through life, Marshbanks, you may have noticed, you make very little impression on the universe. I can scarcely hear your step on the gravel. As you cross the lawn I never see footprints, even when the grass is frosted. You are a drop in the ocean, Marshbanks, a puff in the wind.

TOM: So what are you worrying about?

TRUSCOTT: I'm not worrying in the least. When I look at Edwin I have no doubts. No doubts whatever.

TOM: It's a good many years since you looked at him.

TRUSCOTT: When I look at Edwin I feel I have every reason to be proud of *my* boy.

TOM: It takes very little, you know.

TRUSCOTT: What?

TOM: One small spermatozoon. All the rest, the thousands of wasted organisms might be described, this is as I understand it, as part of nature's bombast, her taste for wild exaggeration.

TRUSCOTT: Do you wish to open the possibility?

TOM: Not a possibility, my Lord. To me it is a certainty.

TRUSCOTT: What?

TOM: Why do you think I'm here for lunch?

TRUSCOTT: To down my sherry, of course. To hack away at my

vintage claret and gobble my duck. 'Second-helping Marsh-banks', that's what Margaret and I call you, behind your back, of course. [*He laughs.*] 'Second-helping'.

TOM: I came here to see my boy.

TRUSCOTT: *My* boy. I don't follow ...

TOM: Come off it, Fen. Could *you* produce a boy that knelt on a church floor, carefully tracing the shapes of dead crusaders, or who sat at an easel on a summer evening, painting the reflections in a reservoir? Could the fruit of *your* old legal loins write poetry, or stand beside me at the kiln and, when the shapes emerged in their perfection, stare breathless at the simplicity of art?

TRUSCOTT: You had *my* Edwin with you, when you were cooking up chamber pots?

TOM: Oh, often on his holidays *my* Edwin came over. He would stay for tea and his mother would join us and we all played *Bohème*. I had Caruso, on the old seventy-eights.

TRUSCOTT: Where was I?

TOM: Hard at work, I imagine, imprisoning people.

TRUSCOTT [*brings his fist down on the arm of his chair*]: I cannot possibly accept this so-called evidence!

TOM: Your wife was there when Edwin span the wheel and made a little mug to take back to school with him. 'Look at the boy's hands,' she'd say. 'He has long artistic fingers, like his father.' Don't look at your hands, Fennimore. Short, stubby fingers, yours, fit for pointing out stab wounds on police photographs.

[*Pause.*]

TRUSCOTT: For the moment ... I suggest we say nothing that would embarrass Margaret.

TOM: Embarrass her?

TRUSCOTT: As for you, Marshbanks ...

TOM: Prisoner at the Bar.

TRUSCOTT: I shall deal with you later.

MARGARET [*calls from inside the conservatory*]: Boys!

[TRUSCOTT *turns in his chair. He sees the shapes of two figures behind the misted green glass.*]

TRUSCOTT: Is that Margaret?

TOM [*turning to look*]: Of course it's Margaret.

TRUSCOTT: Who's that with her? In the conservatory? Can't you see someone? Some shape.

[MARGARET *comes out of the conservatory. We can see another figure standing in the shadows of the conservatory behind her.*]

MARGARET [*to the figure*]: They're sitting there gossiping. Nineteen to the dozen. Under the old mulberry tree. Heaven knows how they find so much to talk about. [*To the two men*] Edwin's here!

[TRUSCOTT *rises in greeting, looking towards the conservatory.*]

TRUSCOTT: *My* son.

TOM [*also rising*]: *My* boy ... Young Edwin!

TRUSCOTT: Well, there you are, Edwin. How are you, my boy?

[*Curtain.*]

END OF SCENE ONE

SCENE TWO

Four o'clock in the afternoon. TRUSCOTT *is in his chair. He is smoking a cigar.* TOM *is sitting also. The sherry decanter has gone, and the tray with glasses.*

TRUSCOTT: Edwin's gone.

TOM: Oh yes. The 'limo' came for him.

TRUSCOTT: The *what*?

TOM: The limousine. Back to Global House.

TRUSCOTT: Yes. Edwin's gone.

TOM: Straight back to London. It seems he's 'got a meeting'.

TRUSCOTT: Which is 'top priority'.

TOM: And which he can't afford to miss. 'Time's money,' says Edwin.

TRUSCOTT: Don't you agree?

TOM: Not money any longer. Time seems to be our dwindling ability to remain alive.

[*Pause.*]

TRUSCOTT: Well, at long last, and after all these years, Edwin has been to luncheon! An opportunity to get to know the boy.

TOM: Not much of an opportunity.

TRUSCOTT: Oh, I don't need long, to get to know the ins and outs of a fellow. In my line of business one gets used to sizing up a witness, fairly quickly. One forms an impression.

TOM: Of course, he's been a long time in Canada. You must make every allowance for that ...

TRUSCOTT: It was good to see the boy again.

TOM: And he didn't make much of an inroad on your sherry.

TRUSCOTT [*thoughtful*]: You noticed that? I noticed it also.

TOM: I think we all noticed.

TRUSCOTT [*disappointed*]: He rejected the Amontillado.

TOM: He asked if we had any 'juice'.

TRUSCOTT: You noticed that too, did you?

TOM: 'Is there a package of juice,' he said, 'in the ice box?'

TRUSCOTT: I was not perfectly clear what the boy was driving at.

TOM: Margaret told him. She told him that the milkman does 'Dayglow Orange Drink' but we hadn't any.

TRUSCOTT: I told him that the Amontillado was juice ... juice of the grape cunningly qualified, but he was having none of it. [*Pause.*] And none of the claret at luncheon, either.

TOM: It seems that Edwin has seen too many people with 'alcohol-related problems'. Among the 'young executives in middle management'.

TRUSCOTT: I used to give Edwin wine for every birthday. On his tenth, as I remember it, I gave him four dozen of the Pichon Longueville ... [*Pause.*] For laying down, not for immediate drinking.

TOM: Immediate drinking, at the age of ten?

TRUSCOTT: When he was eleven I laid down five cases of the Cantenac Beychevelle for Edwin.

TOM: We've made a few inroads on the cellar since then.

TRUSCOTT: Not too many inroads. We'd saved a great deal for the boy. [*Pause.*] Now it seems we've saved it for ourselves. [*Pause.*] He hardly touched his roast duck, did you notice also? Edwin hardly pecked at a drumstick.

TOM: Cholesterol. He said he'd seen too much of that in business.

TRUSCOTT: That was the reason he gave for doing such poor justice to the loganberry pie, and giving the cold shoulder to our cream boat.

TOM: He said he'd seen too many young executives go through the same thing.

TRUSCOTT: Loganberry pie?

TOM: No. Open heart surgery.

TRUSCOTT: Well, really. I've tackled loganberry pie regularly, man and boy, for a good many years.

TOM: And your heart has remained as closed as ever.

TRUSCOTT: Well, I've never been scared of a carving of duck. Let's put it that way, shall we?

TOM: Of course, Edwin said he'd had a good breakfast. He told us that he will always start the day with a dish of breakfast cereal. Don't you remember Edwin telling us that, Fennimore?

TRUSCOTT: Cereal! Is that those small segments of baked cardboard that come in packets? Cereal, it seems, is something Edwin has taken to since he's been away from us.

TOM: Of course, he explained he doesn't really have time for anything else in the mornings. He's always 'in a heck of a hurry getting to Global Computers'.

TRUSCOTT: 'The Company'.

TOM [*starting to laugh*]: He hasn't been doing much log-cabinning, has he? Not much running wild, as you suggested. He's spent ten years in the Global office in Toronto ... rising to the executive floor by 'the sheer damned will to succeed' ...

TRUSCOTT: And I tell you something else! Edwin had absolutely no recollection of ever having rubbed a single brass. Not even when he was of tender years. He simply gave no support of your evidence of 'artistic leanings'. [*Pause.*] It also seems that he never wrote poetry on the subject of the wind.

TOM [*sings*]:

> *'Che gelida manina,*
> *Se la lasci riscaldar.*
> *Cercar che giova ...'*

TRUSCOTT: And he couldn't even remember you playing that damned ditty on your wind-up gramophone!

TOM: Odd that he couldn't remember you bowling leg breaks to him either, down on the edge of the paddock! He never seems to have hit a six into the apple trees – and he couldn't remember a single one of your notable murders.

TRUSCOTT: I asked him what he *did* remember. Well, in all fairness I thought I was bound to put the question.

TOM: He remembered lying on his bed all the afternoon doing algebra.

TRUSCOTT: He said the three of us were always talking together. He preferred his maths, it seems, to our company. [*Pause.*] Of course, I noticed that as a boy Edwin was not always with us. I thought he was behind the shrubbery somewhere, playing pirates.

TOM: In fact he was doing sums!

TRUSCOTT: Training himself for his professional life.

TOM: His intimate knowledge of computers.

TRUSCOTT: Didn't it occur to you that Edwin had a somewhat

exaggerated respect for those no doubt useful little gadgets?

TOM: He told you the law needed one of his 'Global' machines. Put in all the facts and get the appropriate sentence out. That's what Edwin told you. Perhaps he's discovered how to dispense with Judges.

TRUSCOTT: No doubt a computer could manufacture your peasant-style jerries without too much of an effort, Marshbanks. Perhaps you're due to be phased out completely.

TOM: 'Your sentences,' said Edwin, 'were influenced by the amount of port you drank the night before, or whether you'd quarrelled with mother, or if Haversack had peed on the carpet.' They could have replaced you years ago, Fennimore, with a decent calculating machine! [*Pause. He looks towards the conservatory, sees a figure behind the glass.*] Here comes Margaret.

TRUSCOTT [*looking at the conservatory*]: Of course, you're very quick to spot her!

[MARGARET *comes out of the conservatory.*]

MARGARET: Edwin's gone.

TOM: Yes.

TRUSCOTT: It's a bit rum, isn't it, his not coming to see us for all those years.

MARGARET: Oh, he came to see us . . .

TOM: What?

MARGARET: He came to England quite often in the autumn. But that's the time you used to like to go to Dieppe. You both used to like it there, in the autumn.

TOM: So we missed Edwin!

MARGARET: Yes, we missed him. [*She sits in one of the chairs.*]

TOM: I suppose you could say it was our fault, really.

TRUSCOTT: Well, you can't go to Dieppe in August. Gives you sun stroke. [*Pause.*] So we missed Edwin.

MARGARET: Well, yes.

TRUSCOTT: And now he's gone.

MARGARET: He was talking to me just now. He dried up for me. In the kitchen.

TOM: Before the 'limo' came for him?

MARGARET: Yes. He was very helpful in that way. He dried up.

TRUSCOTT: Handle a deft tea towel, does Edwin?

MARGARET: And he was saying that he'd avoided marriage for a good many years.

TOM: He told us that at lunch. He said he'd seen too many 'young executives' with marriage problems. It affected them, he told us. Just when they should be 'maximizing their input for the company'. 'Marriage,' Edwin thinks, 'is one of the chief reasons for divorce.'

TRUSCOTT: It also leads to crime, that's been my experience after a good many years on the Bench.

MARGARET: Well, Edwin seems to have high hopes for his marriage with Arlene.

TRUSCOTT: Whoever's Arlene?

MARGARET: Arlene Jackson. Daughter of the Vice President in charge of Media Promotion . . .

TOM: He never told *us* about Arlene.

TRUSCOTT: Perhaps he thought it was something more suitable for his mother to deal with.

MARGARET: And of course they're getting this house together.

TRUSCOTT: Who are?

MARGARET: Edwin and Arlene.

TRUSCOTT: They'll need one if they're getting married. I don't know what you'd have done without *our* matrimonial home, Marshbanks. You'd have been hard put to it to know where to turn for a free luncheon!

MARGARET: It seems Edwin's being put in charge of the California office. They've got a big house on the beach. Edwin says life's very easy there. The marketing's so simple.

TRUSCOTT: Marketing?

MARGARET: You just drive in and park behind the supermarket and someone will carry it out for you. And it's never cold. The weather's the same every day on the coast, except for a little fog occasionally. [*Pause.*] He thinks this place is too big for us. The garden's too much to keep up, Edwin thinks, and Cattermole's getting too old to cope with it. And one other thing . . .

TRUSCOTT: What other thing?

MARGARET: He thinks you quarrel too much.

TRUSCOTT: Quarrel?

MARGARET: You and Tom quarrel. Edwin says it's not a happy atmosphere. He's worried about me, as his mother.

TRUSCOTT: Well, of course we quarrel.

TOM: Isn't that what neighbours are for?

MARGARET: Edwin finds it strange that you quarrel so much, and then go on holiday together.

TRUSCOTT: So does Edwin offer any solution . . . to this allegedly puzzling situation?

MARGARET: Edwin recommends a change.

TOM: For all of us?

MARGARET: It would amount to that. Edwin wanted me to tell you his idea. He thought that might be better.

TRUSCOTT: Edwin has an idea, has he? A 'wheeze'. Is it something brilliant?

MARGARET: Of course, it would mean putting Gallows Corner on the market.

TRUSCOTT: Gallows Corner to be sold? [*Pause*.] Less than brilliant.

MARGARET: What Edwin said was . . . he felt he had to get nearer to us. That was it! He wanted to come much closer.

TRUSCOTT: Aren't we too old for that?

TOM: He said all this during the washing up?

MARGARET: He feels that he owes it to us to look after us in our old age. He wanted you to consider it carefully.

TRUSCOTT: Consider what, exactly?

MARGARET: Edwin says there's plenty of room in their new house on the coast.

TRUSCOTT: Plenty of room for what?

MARGARET: For his father, and mother of course.

TRUSCOTT: The coast of *what* was it again?

MARGARET: The coast of America. Edwin wants his father to live there too.

TOM: And Arlene.

MARGARET: And Arlene, of course.

[*Pause*.]

TRUSCOTT: He distinctly said he wanted his 'father' to join the happy couple on the coast? That is your clear recollection?

MARGARET: I promised I'd ask you to think about it.

TRUSCOTT: Well, doesn't that pose rather a question?

MARGARET: Yes.

TRUSCOTT: You know, Marshbanks. I have been thinking about young Edwin since he left us this afternoon.

MARGARET: It's getting cold in the garden. Shouldn't we be going indoors?

TRUSCOTT: Edwin wishes his father to join him on 'the coast'. Is that the simple point at issue, Margaret?

MARGARET: Yes. [*She gets up.*] I'm going indoors to put the kettle on. We'll have to light a log fire this evening. [*She moves towards the conservatory.*] Why don't you come in? You've both sat out past any sensible time for sitting.

TRUSCOTT: Presently, Margaret. We'll be in for tea presently.

[MARGARET *goes into the house, through the conservatory, leaving the two men alone together.*]

TOM: Edwin'll look after you in America, Fennimore. He'll probably put you on a diet. Just juice and wheatgerm!

TRUSCOTT: However serious the situation, Marshbanks, you can be relied on to say something entirely trivial. What do you call that – artistic licence?

TOM: Oh, you'll lose weight on the coast, won't you? You'll leave your stomach in San Francisco ...

TRUSCOTT: Do you never glance in the mirror? It's your figure that shows every sign of a lifetime's self-indulgence ... of the grossest sort.

TOM: Steady on, old fellow. No need to get personal.

TRUSCOTT: I don't care for that 'old fellow'. Coming from you, 'old fellow' grates.

[*Pause,* TOM *smiles.*]

TOM: Of course, life in California may change you, Fennimore.

TRUSCOTT: Change me?

TOM: All that lying in the sun. And going barefoot along the beach. Do you think you might become a beachcomber, Fennimore? Wear 'sneakers' and give up shaving?

TRUSCOTT: Oh, Marshbanks. Do be very careful.

TOM: Or take up some ... musical instrument. The guitar perhaps. [*Hardly able to stop laughing.*] Shall we possibly see you on summer nights on the porch, strumming the guitar . . . and tricked out in beads?

TRUSCOTT: There is such a thing as Contempt of Court, you know. Deliberate Contempt, in the face of the tribunal.

[TOM *stands*.]

TOM: I'm going in to tea. [*Pause*.] I forget . . . Am I still on trial? [*He moves away*.]

TRUSCOTT: Still very much on trial. And you would do well to remember it.

[TOM *goes*. TRUSCOTT *sits for a moment in silence*. MARGARET *calls from the house*.]

MARGARET [*off*]: Are you coming, Fen?

[TRUSCOTT *doesn't answer*. *Then* MARGARET *comes out of the conservatory to him*.]

MARGARET: You're missing your tea.

[TRUSCOTT *doesn't answer*.]

MARGARET: Sitting out there any longer you'll miss your tea entirely.

TRUSCOTT: What a tragedy!

MARGARET: Not a tragedy, Fen. But a pity. Perhaps.

TRUSCOTT: There are certain things more important than tea, Margaret. You wouldn't understand that, of course.

MARGARET: I suppose there are. But not many things, I should have thought. Not for us, nowadays. [*She sits in the chair near to him*.]

TRUSCOTT: There are certain things vastly more important.

MARGARET: Oh, I suppose you mean your little trials.

TRUSCOTT: My 'little' trials, as you are pleased to call them . . . are a means to an end. And that end is the truth. Now, as ever, the truth of the matter is vital! Absolutely vital!

MARGARET: Well, you won't find it out with a trial, will you?

TRUSCOTT: A trial in a British court, Margaret, is the one sure way of arriving at the facts.

MARGARET [*smiling*]: Do you really believe that? All that dressing up. And wigs. And long speeches. And people swearing on

Bibles. And tripping each other up with silly questions. Do you really think that ever proves anything?

TRUSCOTT [*grumbling*]: All these long years I've been married to an anarchist.

MARGARET: All it proves is that men like putting on a performance. I've always thought it's got about as much to do with telling the truth as amateur theatricals.

TRUSCOTT [*shocked*]: Amateur theatricals?

MARGARET: I'm sorry, Fen. I didn't mean to hurt your feelings.

TRUSCOTT: You're speaking of matters ... you're quite unqualified to understand.

MARGARET: Oh dear, yes. I suppose I am.

TRUSCOTT: Can you or any other member of the Red persuasion think of a better method of finding out exactly what happened?

[*Pause.*]

MARGARET: Please don't ask me, Fen.

TRUSCOTT: Of course you can't!

MARGARET: You really shouldn't ask me. [*She stands.*] It's not for me to tell you. [*Pause. She looks down at him.*] Anyway. There is one thing.

TRUSCOTT: What?

MARGARET: When you were in Court it never stopped you having your tea. I remember your clerk made Earl Grey in the Judge's room. In the bone china.

TRUSCOTT: Leave me a moment, Margaret. I have matters to consider.

MARGARET: You're not coming in?

TRUSCOTT: Not yet. No.

MARGARET [*moving away*]: Well of course, you must please yourself entirely.

[*As* MARGARET *goes into the conservatory* TRUSCOTT *is left sitting alone. He speaks to the audience as though they were a Jury.*]

TRUSCOTT: Members of the Jury. On the evidence you have heard, you may have no doubt that the prosecution have made out an overwhelming case. I believe there is no alternative to a verdict of guilty on the first count of the indictment. The

charge of the unlawful rogering of Lady Margaret Truscott by
the man Marshbanks has been proved entirely to my satisfaction. I only wish I could say, 'That is the end of the matter',
and discharge you from further deliberation. But one vital
issue still remains. Did that unlawful act cause the birth of a
male child, known to posterity as Edwin Truscott?

[*He turns to look at the conservatory. We see the figures of*
MARGARET *and* TOM *against the greenish glass. We hear the
small sound of their laughter.*]

It is rare, members of the Jury, for us to be able to observe,
during the course of a trial, the accused and his accomplice at
the scene of a crime. I would urge you to take full advantage
of that opportunity. Watch carefully. Are they talking in an
animated manner? You might have thought that at their age,
and after so long an acquaintance, they would have run out of
ordinary innocent conversation. You might have expected the
two of them to have fallen into a decent silence. If they have
not, does it argue a *tête-à-tête* of a most intimate nature? Could
they possibly be discussing Edwin's invitation to join him in
the United States of America? Members of the Jury, the issue
of parentage is always a painful one, but painful issues must
be faced. At this stage of the trial you will not flinch nor fail.
You will soldier on.

[*He sits on for a moment and then rises slowly and walks
towards the conservatory.*]

[*The lights fade to indicate a passage of time and come up again
quickly. The stage is empty.* TRUSCOTT *comes out into the garden
with* TOM.]

TOM: I will say this for old Maggie. She puts on a rattling good
tea.

[TRUSCOTT *sits and starts judicially.*]

TRUSCOTT: I am reminded of a number of different pieces of
evidence, unimportant in themselves perhaps, but fitted
together they add up to an unanswerable case.

TOM: Oh dear. Are we to have another case?

TRUSCOTT: A short one only. And one of which the result may be not unwelcome to you, Thomas.

TOM: You mean I'm not to be condemned to death?

TRUSCOTT: Eventually, of course. But not, perhaps, today.

TOM: Well, Fen, let's hear it.

TRUSCOTT: I would start by reminding you ... [*To himself*] I am sure you will remember the evidence, members of the Jury, with the attention you have clearly been paying throughout this unfortunate case ... [*Aloud*] Edwin takes breakfast cereal.

TOM: *Your* Edwin.

TRUSCOTT: Edwin, I repeat, ingests some pre-packaged preparation on rising. He is also, as it has been admitted, an addict of 'juice'. When faced with a duck drumstick he babbles of cholesterol, when offered a healthy glass of claret, which can only have the effect of raising the spirits and keeping the bowels regular, he is visited by dark thoughts of alcoholism and loss of employment. How would you describe a fellow, Marshbanks, who puts off marriage, as you have put it off?

TOM: Sensible.

TRUSCOTT: 'Sensible' or ... [*With disgust*] would you say 'artistic'? A vegetarian, an addict of free love ... and knickerbockers. Just the sort to indulge himself in brass-rubbings, and water colours, if you want my opinion. A pale and unhealthy youth, if I may charge my recollection, who when the other lads were playing pirates in the orchard, lay up on his bed doing quadratic equations.

TOM [*puzzled*]: Other lads?

TRUSCOTT: An underminer of married life, witness his determined attempt to 'sell up' Gallows Corner.

TOM: Not a sound scheme, that, of Edwin's.

TRUSCOTT: Almost as bad, would you say, as haunting conservatories when a husband's back is turned, as creeping round with a handful of eggs, whistling tender moments from the repertoire of Italian caterwaulers ... Edwin is a chip off the old block, if you ask my opinion.

TOM: A ... What?

TRUSCOTT: Like father like son! Blood may be thicker than water, even though, in the case of the Marshbanks family, it emerges in the form of 'juice'.

TOM: *My* family?

TRUSCOTT: Oh chuck it, Tom. It's clear as mud. He *couldn't* be mine! Edwin is *your* boy!

TOM: My . . .?

TRUSCOTT: Your son! The fruit of your loins. I suppose, given the somewhat spare and skinny nature of the loins in question, the fruit is as sour and meagre as might be expected.

TOM: *My* son? Now look here, Fennimore . . .

TRUSCOTT: Your by-blow! Your little bit of the wrong side of the blanket. A potter's bastard, spawned from a quick clutch in the conservatory, a hasty embrace behind the aspidistras. If anyone has to go and live on 'the coast' it should certainly be you!

TOM: I begin to see what's happening. A miscarriage of justice! No, *you* go, Fennimore. He's your responsibility!

TRUSCOTT: As you hinted, Edwin is a sensitive plant. Takes after his father. Of course he wrote to you from Lawnhurst. What did you send your sprig, Marshbanks, a hot water bottle and a couple of chest protectors?

TOM: Edwin, if you want my opinion, has not got the soul of an artist.

TRUSCOTT: But he's got the artist's infallible instinct for winkling respectable people out of their homes.

TOM: What artist has ever been known to lie on his bed doing quadratic equations?

TRUSCOTT: Suppose you tell me. Wasn't the poet Shelley a bit of a one for the higher mathematics?

TOM: The poet Shelley, you can take it from me, Fennimore, had never even heard of algebra.

TRUSCOTT: You're sure?

TOM: The main characteristic of young Edwin . . .

TRUSCOTT: Not so young.

TOM: Of Edwin, I would say, is his grasp of business matters, his lack of imagination, the plodding, not to say pedantic manner in which he expresses himself. In any conceivable cricket team of crashing bores, *your* Edwin would undoubtedly be first in to bat.

TRUSCOTT: *My* Edwin? Oh, do be very careful, Marshbanks. Did you say *my* Edwin, by any chance?

TOM: With a bore of that magnitude, there's bound to be a lawyer in his pedigree. Besides, Edwin could never be anything as interesting as a bastard. That young man was conceived with the utmost respectability ... one night, perhaps, when you had become overexcited by a day spent imposing deterrent sentences and Maggie closed her eyes and hummed Puccini to herself.

TRUSCOTT: Oh, be careful!

TOM: What will you get me for. Contempt of Court?

TRUSCOTT: Could I have given birth to a boy who rejected the Pichon Longueville?

TOM: Oh, easily. You believe in character-building, don't you? In self-discipline. Free will and taking the tough decision. Well, *your* boy Edwin has just disciplined himself out of a decent wine. Anyway, he looks like you.

TRUSCOTT: Like me! Put him up to the light and you could see through him.

TOM: Before you grew that stomach and your nose went purple, he's the spitting image.

TRUSCOTT: Of you, Marshbanks. Put a spotted bow tie round the boy's neck and he'd look every inch a potter!

TOM: A lawyer, Fennimore. Every inch a lawyer.

TRUSCOTT: Nonsense!

TOM: A development, of course, since your vintage. Edwin is 'le Truscott nouveau', a fresh and impertinent young wine with a greatly increased boring factor.

TRUSCOTT: Not a Truscott! 'Nouveau' or anything else.

[TRUSCOTT *gets up, moves to look at the garden.* TOM *also rises and follows him.*]

TOM: Edwin is your gift to the future, Fennimore. The man who makes his decisions with a machine, with no small error of mercy possible.

TRUSCOTT: He's a bloody vegetarian brass-rubber.

TOM: Rubbish. Anyway, *I'm* not a vegetarian.

TRUSCOTT: You're a duck-gobbling, poultry-eating vegetarian!

TOM: There is only one thing to be said for Edwin. He is clearly not my responsibility!

TRUSCOTT: Nothing's your responsibility, is it? That's what's wrong with you, Marshbanks. I've heard it a thousand times. 'I don't know what made me do it, my Lord.' You know quite well what made you do it. A taste for rogering married ladies! And now you must simply face up to the appalling consequences of your actions!

[*Pause.* TOM *looks at the conservatory. There seem to be shapes behind the glass.*]

TOM: Is that Maggie ... up there in the conservatory?

TRUSCOTT: A brief spasm of so-called delight, and a lifetime of Edwin to look forward to. Given his ridiculous anxiety to remain alive he'll probably reach ninety.

TOM: Is there someone up there in the conservatory, with Maggie?

TRUSCOTT [*looking towards the conservatory*]: Probably Edwin.

TOM: Edwin left to go back to London.

TRUSCOTT: To go back to Global Computers. Yes.

TOM: She must be alone then. It's the shape, the shadows on that green glass that are confusing.

[*The conservatory door opens.* MARGARET *comes out alone.*]

MARGARET [*moving towards them*]: Still out there chattering! Whatever do you two find to talk about?

TRUSCOTT: Something about which we would like your honest ... opinion. Sit down for a moment. [*He sits.*] Please ... make yourself comfortable, madam.

TOM [*warning*]: Fennimore! [*He sits.*]

TRUSCOTT: It's no good, Marshbanks. We can't live forever in a state of suspended speculation. The time has come when a decision has to be reached, however painful.

MARGARET: What is it now? Has Haversack been digging in the flower beds again?

TOM: No, Maggie. It's not Haversack.

TRUSCOTT: I'm afraid the issues raised here are rather more serious.

MARGARET: More serious than Haversack digging in the new rose bed? There's a last little splash of sunshine. I will sit with you, just for a few moments. [*She sits.*]

TRUSCOTT: I will now call Lady Margaret Truscott.

MARGARET: I'm here, Fennimore. You don't need to call me.

TRUSCOTT: I had hoped to deal with this matter without troubling you to give evidence, without you having to recall facts of a no doubt painful and embarrassing nature.

MARGARET: And for supper, I thought cold cuts, on a tray in front of the fire.

TRUSCOTT: Madam. The allegations that have been brought against me personally are of such a grave nature that the matter must be cleared up now, before any adjournment is granted.

MARGARET: I know no law. I really can't join in your game. Shan't we all go in?

TRUSCOTT: Until my name is cleared, we do not go in!

MARGARET: What is it, Tom? Can you understand him?

TOM: Oh yes, Maggie. I can understand.

TRUSCOTT: I leave aside the questionable behaviour of this man Marshbanks. I pass no judgement on whether or not and in what precise circumstances you were rogered by him.

MARGARET [sighs]: Oh, Fen dear. Not that again.

TRUSCOTT: The present position is far more serious. The charge is that I fathered the person Edwin. That I, Sir Fennimore Truscott, Q.C., one of Her Majesty's Judges of the Queen's Bench, retired and put out to grass, did maliciously burden the future with the said person, thereby diminishing, to that extent, the quality of life on earth.

TOM: Tell him, Maggie. Who was Edwin's father?

MARGARET: Do you wish it were you?

TOM: No. Quite honestly.

MARGARET: Neither of you wants him. [Pause. She stands.] Come on, boys. Let's go indoors.

TRUSCOTT: Not until you have answered my question.

MARGARET: How can I make you understand?

TRUSCOTT: I propose to call Lady Margaret Truscott. I assume the witness wishes to affirm.

MARGARET: Affirm what?

TRUSCOTT: Being of the Red persuasion she wishes to swear to the truth in some mealy-mouthed secular fashion.

MARGARET: I don't know why I should have the responsibility . . .

TOM: What we want to know quite simply, Maggie, is *which* of us?

TRUSCOTT: Which of us is responsible for what I suppose might be called the 'younger generation' who may or may not, in the course of time, inherit our bits and pieces. [*Pause.*] To me Edwin has the distinct smell of a Marshbanks to him.

TOM: To me he is all Truscott.

MARGARET [*moving away to look at the garden*]: Edwin. My son.

TRUSCOTT: On *that* issue there can be no room for doubt, I imagine.

TOM: No doubt he wants *you* to go out there, Maggie?

MARGARET: He meant it well, I'm sure, when he invited me.

TOM: What did you say? I mean, what were *your* feelings, exactly?

MARGARET: Oh, I told him I couldn't go. I had to get the geraniums in. On the coast, it seems, the geraniums may stay out all of the year round. 'Well,' I said, 'that doesn't leave much for a gardener to do.'

TOM: What did Edwin say to that?

MARGARET: 'Geraniums,' he told me, 'are not everything. The future is out there on the coast,' he said. Quite honestly, Edwin can't find the future here.

TOM: Can he not? What have you done with the future, Fen?

TRUSCOTT: You're not going with him, are you, Margaret?

[*Pause.*]

MARGARET: If I thought of it . . . I'd have to talk the matter over with Edwin's father.

TOM: But you've done that, Maggie!

MARGARET: No. I don't think I could. It would cause embarrassment. I'm not sure his wife would like it.

TOM: His wife?

TRUSCOTT: I'm not quite catching the drift of this evidence . . .

[MARGARET *moves back towards them.*]

MARGARET: Edwin talks about the future. Well, I certainly wasn't thinking about the future . . . not that summer before the year when Edwin was born.

TOM: A good summer, as I remember, particularly in the soft fruit department.

MARGARET: Every day starting with the sun melting the mist over the herbaceous border. It seems to me, looking back on it, a time of love ... [*She sits.*]

TRUSCOTT: Quite clearly of love, among other crimes.

TOM: Go on ...

MARGARET: I loved you, Tom, because you were so strong and independent. Tough as old boots, caring about your pots and the rest of the world could go hang as far as you were concerned.

TRUSCOTT: Tom? Strong? I can't say I follow the drift of this evidence.

MARGARET: And you, Fen, because of that ridiculous vulnerability ...

TRUSCOTT: Perhaps, madam, you're not feeling quite yourself.

MARGARET: You cared so desperately about what people thought. You wanted to please everyone.

TRUSCOTT: *Everyone!*

MARGARET: The police officers, and the Jury. I used to see you in Court, trying to seduce the Jury. I think you even tried to flatter the criminals by pretending their little crimes were so desperately important.

TOM [*laughing*]: She's caught you neatly, Fen!

TRUSCOTT: I hope we may be coming to a less frivolous part of the evidence ...

MARGARET: I mean, you may love someone ... you may love the way they spin a potter's wheel with such outrageous confidence, or go to work at the Law Courts each morning trembling with fear and trying to put a ridiculously brave face on it. And you may love the way someone prunes roses, stooping so easily, or weeds the strawberry bed all day in the hot sunshine ... with the dark stain of sweat growing on the back of his shirt.

TOM: I'm lost. Do you prune roses, Fennimore?

TRUSCOTT: Never. Neither do you. That's a job we always leave to Cattermole. Cattermole's the expert.

TOM: Cattermole?

MARGARET: But just because you love someone, just because one summer ... Well, I can't see that I'm responsible ...

TOM: And wasn't it Cattermole who, more often than not, weeded the strawberry bed ...?

MARGARET: Just because I may have laid myself down from time to time that summer ...

TRUSCOTT: In the conservatory?

MARGARET: Oh ... the orchard or the conservatory. I can't remember everything.

TRUSCOTT: Oh try, madam. Do your best to charge your recollection.

MARGARET: What I mean is ...

TRUSCOTT: Yes, madam. Tell us exactly what you do mean. So that we may note it down.

[*There seems to be a figure in the conservatory, vaguely outlined against the glass.*]

MARGARET: I mean, just because you fancy the way a man stands patiently pricking out seed boxes, that doesn't make you responsible, does it, for the future?

TOM: What are you trying to tell us, Maggie?

MARGARET: To tell you? [*Small laugh*] Don't both look so solemn. [*Pause.*] How could we have run this great place, without Cattermole to help us out? [*Pause. She gets up and moves towards the conservatory.*] I'm going in now. Up to the house. I'm cold and I really can't tell you any more about it.

[*She goes into the conservatory. We seem to see two figures.*]

TOM: She's gone.

TRUSCOTT: Up to the house?

TOM: Into the conservatory.

[*They both look at the conservatory.*]

TRUSCOTT: Can you see her? We must get that glass cleaned occasionally. Now I can see her. I can see a shape.

TOM: *One* shape, Fennimore. Is that all you can see?

TRUSCOTT: Yes, I think so. I honestly think so.

[*The shapes behind the conservatory glass move away. It looks empty.*]

TRUSCOTT: What was Margaret saying about our jobbing gardener, Cattermole? I'm not entirely sure I got the drift of her evidence.

TOM: Are you not, Fennimore? Are you really not sure?

TRUSCOTT [*resigned*]: Well, then. I suppose I am. [*Pause.*] The sun's dropped down behind the herbaceous border. Time to go in?

TOM: Well, yes. I suppose it is.

[TRUSCOTT *stands up.*]

TRUSCOTT: You'll stay for supper, won't you, Marshbanks?

[TOM *gets up.*]

TOM: You really want me . . .?

TRUSCOTT [*laughs*]: 'Second-helping Marshbanks'. The unfortunate fact is . . . I'm not sure we can do without you.

[*The two men move towards the conservatory together.*]

TRUSCOTT: One thing to be thankful for. Edwin has left us a bottle or two. Shall we have time, I wonder, to get through it all?

TOM: Edwin! What do you think honestly? Is Edwin the future?

TRUSCOTT: Not ours, Tom. Let's thank God for it. Not ours!

[*They go into the conservatory, and on into the house together.*]

The curtain falls.

BERMONDSEY

Bermondsey was first produced at the New Theatre, London, on 27 January 1970 with the following cast:

IRIS PURVIS	*Glynis Johns*
BOB PURVIS	*Joss Ackland*
PIP LESTER	*Denholm Elliott*
ROSEMARY	*Pauline Collins*

Scene: The living room behind the bar in the Purvis's pub – the Cricketers, Bermondsey.

Time: Christmas Eve, after closing time.

The Purvis's living room, behind the bar of the Cricketers in Bermondsey. Peeling three-piece suite, wallpaper with pattern of Windsor Castle, ashtrays and calendar advertising 'Take Courage'. Christmas decorations. In the centre of the room, a Christmas tree, trimmed. The presents are set round: boxes in gold paper, unexpectedly large and lush. Christmas drinks: large selection on a table. Upright piano with carol book on it, open. When the curtain rises, the stage is empty. Sound of voices, children being put to bed upstairs. A young girl, blonde, mini-skirted and carrying a tray with two children's mugs on it comes in from the kitchen. She looks calm, in control, unhurried when a voice calls at her from upstairs.

IRIS: Rosemary? . . . Rosemary?
ROSEMARY: Yes, Mrs Purvis?
IRIS [*calls from off*]: Got the kids' hot drinks, have you?
ROSEMARY: Just coming.
BOB [*ad lib – off*]: Good night. Happy Christmas, etc.

> [BOB PURVIS *walks in from the bar. He's big, handsome, about thirty-eight. His life in the pub is starting to make him overweight.*]

ROSEMARY: Don't know what your wife thinks she is – Shah of bloody Persia.
BOB [*ignoring this*]: Taking that up to the kids, are you?
ROSEMARY: When're you going to tell her, Bob?
BOB: After Christmas. I'll tell her after the holiday.
ROSEMARY: Boxing day. Promise you'll tell her . . .? [*She starts to go upstairs.*]
BOB: Of course I promise. After the holiday.

> [*She goes.*
> PIP LESTER *comes in from the empty bar. He's thin, sharp featured, grey round the temples, rather high upper-class voice, pianist's hands and gestures, dressed with perpetual undergraduate untidiness. Shapeless grey trousers, tweed coat with*

leather patches, old khaki shirt, straying lock of hair, slightly loping walk. He looks after ROSEMARY, *doubtful and suspicious.*]

PIP [*feeling his arm*]: I'm out of practice, pulling beer handles.

BOB: Why not open the shampoo, boy? That's what you're used to.

  [PIP *moves to the drinks tables, opens champagne.*]

PIP: Children gone to bed, have they?

BOB: Iris never gets them off till past closing time – not on Christmas Eve.

PIP: Care for a glass of the old shampoo? [*He pours himself a gin.*]

BOB: Go ahead. I'll stick to the Mother's Ruin. Shampoo gets my gut.

PIP [*the cockney phrase carefully mixed with the upper-class accent*]: Iris likes a drop of the old shampoo. [*He pours a gin for* BOB.]

BOB: Yes, Iris likes it.

PIP: The kids look smashing. [*He takes* BOB *his gin, then he looks at the big boxes round the tree.*] I hope my presents'll be a success.

  [*Noise from above.*]

BOB: Cheeky little buggers. They're playing up.

PIP [*pats wrapped presents*]: One Junior road-scorcher two-wheel Fire-Fly for Ronnie – and a rather impertinent looking person called 'Miss Isobel' who brings up her own wind for Carol Anne.

BOB: You spoil them!

PIP: Nonsense. I'm spoiling myself. Trying to make up for what I've missed. [*He goes back to the table – takes his champagne.*]

BOB: You've not missed a thing. Iris says she can't switch on Late Night Line Up but you're chatting away about Brahms, or whatever . . .

  [*Pause.*
  PIP *drinks, looks at* BOB.]

PIP: Bob?

BOB: Yes?

PIP: Do you know how long it's gone on?

BOB: Since I married Iris? I was trying to reckon the other day. Ronnie's just eleven ...

PIP: No. I mean ... *it*.

BOB: Oh, 'it'. 'It's' what you're talking about.

PIP: Eighteen years!

BOB: You're joking!

PIP: Eighteen years exactly. Since we stood on that horrible Parade Ground ... With Dulcie Dubbin screaming her head off at us ...

BOB: Our camp Sergeant! [*Remembering, imitating shrill Sergeant's voice.*] 'When I says "Fix" – yer don't fix!'

PIP [*same imitation – not so good*]: 'But when I says "Bayonets" – yer pops them off and yer whops them on!'

BOB: When we was on an exercise near this bloody great castle, and Dulcie says 'This here's the property of Lady Thaxted. Mind your fairy footprints on the turf, you clumsy bastards.' And you said – 'Sergeant – she's my mother, and she'd like you all to come in to Christmas dinner.'

PIP: My mother's splendid, in national emergencies. She spent the war preparing an icy calm welcome for the German Commandant who never turned up.

BOB: Bit of an anti-climax then, a peacetime invasion of National Service yobs.

PIP: That was the first time I ever played the piano to you. Remember, when Mother got the others on to Animal Grab?

BOB: You dragged me off into the Music Room. I thought you'd never stop. I thought, how the shit do I ask him to belt up, and then we got started on the whisky and the Christmas carols. Is that eighteen years, honestly? Well, I'll say this, Pip. You've done all right for yourself since then, boy.

PIP: Not really. You've had all the great events.

BOB [*sarcastic*]: Oh, yes! We just live on excitement here in the Cricketers. Do you know what happened? Just in the last three months?

PIP: I haven't been down. Not since Iris's birthday.

BOB: Was that when you brought her – a bottle of pong from the both of us?

PIP: Giant-sized Balmain 'Jolie Madame'. With a joke card from you to put your name to . . .

BOB: You see! Things only happen when you call on us! Since then, well, since then . . . We had Iris's Mum for one God awful weekend. Carol Anne got a pain in her gut which let everyone down by not being appendicitis . . . And oh, young Rosemary came to help Iris out. Ex-National Service Corporal Robert Purvis – This is your bleeding existence . . .

[*He drinks* . . . PIP *laughs, drinks to him.*]

PIP [*a little anxious*]: Yes. Well, about . . . Rosemary?

BOB: Iris needed someone to help out.

PIP: Did she?

BOB: She's not a bad young girl. Had some trouble at home. Of course, Iris has to show her everything.

PIP: I noticed that.

BOB: But we do a lot more trade since her mini-skirt erupted in the saloon . . . [*Pause. He goes on, more confidential*] Also, she's set me thinking . . .

PIP [*laughs at him*]: Sounds bad!

BOB: No! No, it's been so long since I got talking to anyone as young as that – I don't count the kids, of course.

PIP: Of course.

BOB: And she got me thinking. Well, I'm in a bit of a rut, here, quite frankly, Pip. I mean, it's no use waking up and finding you've missed the bus, is it?

PIP: What bus exactly?

[*He goes to the piano and starts to play 'The Holly and the Ivy'. He's playing standing up and sings.* BOB *moves and stands close to him.* PIP *plays.*]

BOB [*puts a hand on* PIP's *shoulder*]: Wasn't that the bloody tune?

PIP: . . . Remember?

BOB: Your Mum brought up Scotch in a decanter. She shoved it on the piano.

PIP: You've got a retentive memory!

BOB: We got pissed out of our minds, and sung that bloody thing all the way back to barracks. You're right, boy. It's retentive all right.

[PIP *suddenly stops playing. The two men face each other, move closer –* BOB's *hand still on* PIP's *shoulder.* PIP *speaks very quietly.*]

PIP: It's only eighteen years.

[*At the same moment they lean forward and kiss each other on the mouth.*
Sound of a door banging and IRIS's *voice on the stairs.*]

IRIS [*off*]: Quiet now, kids. Or Santa's not going to come. Not ever.

[*The men move apart, not hurriedly.* IRIS *comes in. She's the perfect pub wife: sensible, still attractive, tired from an evening in the bar and putting the kids to bed. She hardly looks at the men, but goes to the tree and straightens the silver ornament on the top of it.*]

IRIS: Can't ever get that old fairy to stand upright.
BOB: Stuff a twig up her.

[*Pause. Sound of children upstairs.*]

IRIS [*hearing it*]: That girl's useless with the kids.

[PIP *pours a glass of champagne and brings it to her.*]

PIP: Shampoo, love?
BOB [*casual*]: Rosemary – still up there, is she?
IRIS: Putting her eyelashes on. Apparently there was an accident in the bar. She left her other pair in an empty glass, and Mrs Beasley poured in a port and lemon and drank them down.
BOB: Silly old fool ...
PIP: How revolting!
IRIS: I said what do you want to take them off in the bar for anyway, and she said – they get so heavy. After a long evening. She doesn't care if our regular barmaid gets a hairy lining to her stomach.
BOB: She's all right. She had a bit of trouble at home.

IRIS: I said, I should think they do get heavy, I said, with all that fluttering you do. She's hopeless with the kids.

BOB: Ronnie likes her.

IRIS: Carol Anne can't stand the sight of her.

BOB: Well, then – Carol Anne's a woman, isn't she?

IRIS: She's six!

BOB: It doesn't matter she's six. She's still a woman, isn't she? She's jealous. That's all. She's jealous of a bit of mini-skirt.

IRIS: Is that what I am! Jealous of *her*.

BOB: I should rather think so. The way you're criticizing.

IRIS: It's just that she's meant to be helping me out.

BOB: Oh, for God's sake, girl. Where's the spirit of Christmas . . .?

IRIS: Drunk up by you, I should imagine. You must've got through one bottle of Gordon's since we opened.

BOB: I've been working . . .

IRIS: What do you think I've been doing? And trailing round after a girl who's got no more sense than to let our bar parlour staff drink down parts of her anatomy . . .

BOB: Give it a rest, Iris. Pip's here.

IRIS: Of course. Pip's here. Pip's always here! Christmas, birthdays. One of the family! [*She empties her glass.*]

BOB: Well, be grateful. You're swigging down his shampoo.

IRIS: Oh, Pip understands. You understand how it is, don't you, Pip?

PIP [*crosses to* IRIS. *Fills her glass again. Looks at* BOB]: Yes, dear. Of course, I understand.

IRIS: And what do *you* think of Miss Mini-Skirt exactly, Pip?

BOB: She's just a young kid – that's got into a bit of trouble at home . . .

IRIS: No. What do *you* think of her Pip?

PIP [*pauses. He's in difficulties, he answers with tact*]: Charming. She's just not – my type exactly . . .

[*Crash from upstairs.*]

BOB: I'd better go up, before the kids commit murder.

[*He goes.* IRIS *shrugs her shoulders.*]

IRIS: What do we do now? Sit in suspense until she drops the other eyelash?

[*She drops into a chair, kicks off her shoes. Drinks.* PIP *comes over and fills her glass.*]

PIP: You're tired.
IRIS: Bloody fed up.

[PIP *goes to the piano. Starts to play 'The Holly and the Ivy' quietly through this dialogue.*]

IRIS [*after a pause*]: How's your mother?
PIP: Indestructible!
IRIS: Shouldn't you be with her at Christmas? Isn't that your place – in the Castle?
PIP: Rheumatism Towers ...
IRIS: Doesn't she miss you?
PIP: She's happy as a sandboy. She's sitting in front of a roaring electric fire, wrapped in two cardigans, fur boots, and the sari they wove for her in Delhi, playing consequences with the local M.P. 'Malcolm Muggeridge met Diana Dors in the Sauna Bath at the Vatican and the consequence was ...'
IRIS: Is that what they play ...?
PIP: My mother always loved paper games with politicians ...
IRIS: Your old Mum. She's certainly part of history. Something like the Bloody Tower. [*Long pause.*] Of course, I know really – why you want to come here. [*He stops playing abruptly. Listens tense.*]
PIP: Why?
IRIS: You're a bit of a snob, aren't you?
PIP [*gets up, puzzled, offended, but relieved*]: *Me!* A snob.
IRIS: Take a trip round the stately pubs of Jamaica Road. Pay your half-crown and catch a glimpse of the 'real people'.
PIP: Iris, that's not fair!
IRIS: Oh, I've seen you. When Carol Anne puts sauce on her bread, your eyes light up as if you'd had a personal invitation to watch the Duke of Edinburgh eat his cucumber sandwiches ...
PIP: Iris, that's just not true!
IRIS: I know what you say about Bob – 'salt of the earth. No nonsense. Real true person.' I don't know what you thought

you'd met. Jesus Christ, just because he'd never seen a pair of pyjamas till he did his National Service ...

PIP: It's all of you. This family ... In the world I live in, there's no real feeling of a family any more ...

IRIS: That's a load of cobblers ... You don't think we're more real, do you – just because we have to make do with an Anglia instead of an Aston Martin, and vinyl instead of wall to wall carpeting. Just because we go on holiday in Hayling Island instead of borrowing old Lucy So-and-so's bloody Greek island.

PIP: Personally – yes I do.

IRIS: Why?

PIP: You're tired ...

IRIS: *Why?* Tell me why – what's so good about us you have to drive down here with champagne and Paris perfume, and walking, talking, peeing dolls. Just as if you were the Three Wise Men and I was the blessed virgin.

PIP [*trying to explain*]: It's because ... Honestly, it's because you're simple.

IRIS: Thank you very much!

PIP: I mean, you don't make great demands on life ...

IRIS [*she gets up, impatient and restless*]: What? Can't you hear? Bob's shouting all the time to be the twenty-five-year-old millionaire owner of the fifty-storey de luxe Happy-Home holiday hotel, Torquay. You don't think the poor fact he's thirty-eight, and the tenant of a small tied house in the Jamaica Road makes any difference to what he's demanding, do you?

PIP: What about you?

IRIS: Oh, what I'm asking for's much more ridiculous.

PIP: What?

[*Pause.*]

IRIS: Love.

[*Pause.*]

PIP: You've got so much.

IRIS: Have I?

PIP: You've got Bob and ...

IRIS: Have I got him?

PIP: And the children ...

IRIS: Is that what you care about?

PIP: My Godchildren? Yes. Yes, of course. I mean, they must be very satisfying.

IRIS: A couple of accidents! If you want to know the truth.

PIP: Iris. I always thought of you as a perfect mother ...

IRIS: That's what perfect mothers get landed with. Accidents.

PIP: I'm afraid I don't know much about it.

IRIS: That's not an area of scientific knowledge that really appeals to you, is it?

PIP: Perhaps not.

IRIS: I bet your greatest nightmare's being stuck here one week-end when I suddenly gave birth, and you have to rush in with boiling water.

PIP: Look, Iris. I don't want to seem old-fashioned. But it's Christmas Eve. We've decorated the tree. The children are asleep upstairs, and I personally thought we should practise the carol for tomorrow ... [*He goes back to the piano, and standing plays a few bars of 'The Holly and the Ivy'.*]

IRIS: Kids! They don't need us. You know what I seem to hear those kids saying all the time? 'We're just an excuse for you, aren't we? All you need us for is to keep your mind off the real trouble.'

PIP [*stops playing again*]: What's that? [*Pause.*] What's the real trouble?

IRIS: Naturally, it's Bob.

PIP: What's the matter with Bob?

IRIS: What's the matter with *you*? You know what's going on ...

PIP: He just seems a bit restless.

IRIS: Restless! Look – [*She stands looking at him.*] You love him, don't you?

[*Long pause.*]

PIP: I've always been very fond of Bob.

IRIS [*impatient*]: Why can't you tell the truth sometimes?

PIP: Well, I do love him – naturally. As a friend ...

IRIS: Oh yes, like you love your Mum. Like you love me. Like you're going to put 'With loads of love from Uncle Pip' on Ronnie's two wheeler.

PIP: Well ... Perhaps not exactly like that.

IRIS: How?

PIP: Well ...

IRIS: Go on, say it. How?

PIP: Well, I suppose ...

IRIS: For God's sake. Do me the credit!

PIP: What?

IRIS: I'm not a complete bloody idiot. I mean I've got some idea
– what's going on. He's your boy friend, isn't he?

[PIP *does a dramatic gesture, his head in his hands.*]

PIP: What do you mean exactly?

IRIS: I never know ... quite how to describe it.

PIP: I'm sorry.

IRIS: Look. It seems perfectly natural to me. It's the people that
don't fancy him I can't understand.

PIP: I won't come again.

IRIS: You've got to.

PIP: I'll stay away.

IRIS: I don't think we could do without you.

PIP: What're you talking about?

IRIS: The way I look at it is – you've kept this family together.

PIP [*incredulously*]: *I* have?

IRIS: You've kept Bob steady. [*Losing patience*] Do you think
I'd've had a peaceful home to bring up the children and a good
husband and holidays, if Bob hadn't had you as well to keep
him feeling young and handsome as a boy of twenty?

PIP [*pauses. He looks at her*]: When did you work it out?

IRIS: Oh, I've known ever since you first took us out. Remember
you got seats for the Victoria Palace? You said, 'May I say how
greatly I admire your hat?'

PIP [*desperate, embarrassed*]: Look, Iris, my car's outside. On
second thoughts, Mother may be feeling a bit low this Christmas, and I really think I should ... [*Turning on her, anxious*]
How could you tell?

IRIS: You were so polite to me.

PIP: Just because I happened to appreciate your hat ...

IRIS: Do you imagine any of the other men we'd known'd say 'I
greatly admire your hat?' They'd pile beside me in the back

of the Anglia and try for a quick grope any time Bob had his eye on the road. [*She drinks.*]

PIP: What I can't understand is, why didn't you object before?

IRIS: Why should I object? I tell you. I knew what Bob was like. I chose him like that, didn't I?

PIP: And I don't make you jealous?

IRIS: You're not jealous of me, are you?

PIP [*thinking it over*]: No. I'm grateful to you, for looking after him.

IRIS: Well, I think you make a nice day out for Bob like going to the dogs, but less expensive ...

PIP: Thank you very much. But ... Why suddenly ... bring it up?

IRIS: Have some sense! Can't you see what's happening to Bob? ... I thought you loved him?

PIP: You know that, apparently ...

IRIS: But you don't, do you? He's just the little bit of rough trade you took in to show round the Castle.

PIP: Iris, please!

IRIS: All right. If you care about him, why don't you put up a bit of a fight then?

PIP: Against you?

IRIS: Against her.

PIP: Her?

IRIS: Little Miss Eyelashes.

PIP: You're jealous of her. I believe you're jealous.

IRIS: Of course, I'm bloody jealous.

PIP: Why?

IRIS: Because she's a woman. And because she's nothing to do with Bob. She's not part of him. She's all in his mind, like the girls he gets on the brewery calendar, unzipping their jeans on black leather sofas. It's all a great big dream, and they'll take on a pub they can't afford, and put on dinners she can't cook and get brewery bills they can't pay, and it wouldn't be one bottle a day – but two and a treble before breakfast and you've got to put a stop to it. You've got to break it up, Pip dear. Before that girl takes my husband off both of us.

PIP: How can I?

IRIS: Tell her! Tell her he's queer.

ROSEMARY [*off*]: 'Night, 'night, Ronnie.

[PIP *is stunned by this suggestion, when* ROSEMARY *comes in downstairs. She's put on enormous eyelashes and she's changed her clothes. She's carrying the emptied children's mugs on the tray.*]

ROSEMARY: I'm not butting in, am I, Mrs Purvis?

IRIS: Not if I can help it, dear. Everything all right up there, then?

ROSEMARY: Oh yes. Mr Purvis was telling the kids a story. It was a scream. Shall I rinse these out under the tap?

IRIS: That's very sweet of you, dear.

[ROSEMARY *goes.*]

You see? In eleven years, he's never told those kids a bedtime story. It's got serious ...

PIP: Bob wouldn't be thinking of – leaving home, would he?

IRIS: If he does, I don't see her having you down for the holidays. [*She looks at him.*] Of course, we could always spend our Christmases together. Just you and me and the kids.

PIP: Perhaps ... You're right.

IRIS: She's got to be told ...

PIP: Then, shouldn't you tell her?

IRIS: She'd never believe me. I'm just the old jealous cow, that's all I am. You see that, don't you, Pip dear? She'd never believe me.

[BOB *comes down the stairs, his hair brushed neatly.*]

BOB: Well, got that lot into bed at last.

IRIS: Including our little Rosemary?

BOB: Sorry, Pip, the kids were just that bit excited.

IRIS [*exasperated*]: What did you do? Calm them down with the one about the poor girl who lost her eyelashes dancing with Prince Charming who whipped her out of the Public Bar and made her sweetheart of the Forces.

BOB: I'm sick and tired of that.

IRIS: What exactly?

BOB: You getting at me. That's all you do now. Just get at me.

PIP [*embarrassed*]: Isn't this the time we always have our Irish coffee? Christmas Eve.

IRIS: She won't know how to do Irish coffee – not that plastic daffodil out there. Most she knows is how to open crisps.

PIP [*anxious to escape*]: Shall I go and do it? Shall I go and do it?

IRIS: Why not. You could probably tell her quite a lot . . . About the way we do things here.

[PIP *goes*.]

IRIS [*to* BOB]: You want to leave us, don't you?

BOB: I was going to tell you, after the holiday.

IRIS: Why not now?

BOB: I didn't want to spoil your Christmas.

IRIS [*seriously*]: Thank you.

BOB [*collects himself for an outburst, and then explodes*]: I want a different sort of place, that's all. By the river, where I could put on prawn cocktails, and charcoal grills and not just rest content with meat pies and cheese biscuits. Somewhere you could put on a dinner dance – for the younger marrieds. I'm getting on, Iris, I'm thirty bloody six. Well, don't I deserve it?

IRIS: You weren't thinking of including me? Not in the move?

BOB [*weak and apologetic*]: I want a bit of something young around me.

[*Pause*.]

IRIS: Thirty-eight.

BOB: What?

IRIS: You're thirty-eight.

BOB: You see, I'm not getting any younger.

IRIS: Neither am I.

BOB [*guilt making him angry*]: Oh, don't try that. I can see that coming. Bloody blackmail. So I've got to stay because I feel sorry for you, is that it? You want me to pity you?

IRIS: No.

BOB: What?

IRIS: Have a bit of pity on yourself.

BOB: I'm no good. I know that.

IRIS: Yes, you are then.

BOB: What?

IRIS: Good. That's why we both love you.

BOB: You and Rosemary . . .?

IRIS: No. You know I don't mean *that*. Me and Pip! We've got good taste – both of us. We like you as you are. If you'd been meant as the guv'ner of a dinner dance Country Club, that's what you'd be by now.

[*The door opens.* ROSEMARY *comes in; she looks extremely puzzled.*]

ROSEMARY: 'Ere, he wants the Irish whiskey. Where is it, Bob?

BOB: Top shelf – up with the liqueurs and specials.

ROSEMARY: He says he's about to do miraculous things, with cream and Irish whiskey. [*She goes off into the bar*.]

IRIS: It's too late, Bob. You can't go back and have it all different . . .

BOB: Keep me down! All right! Just keep me down all the time! Can't I have a bit of ambition?

IRIS: If anyone's achieved their ambitions I'd say it was you.

BOB: Gordon Bennett! I've had less out of life than anyone.

IRIS: At a modest estimate, I'd say you've had – about twice as much.

[ROSEMARY *comes back from the bar carrying the Irish whiskey. She speaks to* BOB, *nods towards the kitchen*.]

ROSEMARY: Who is he, Bob?

BOB: Just an old friend, that's all.

ROSEMARY: He said you had a whole lot of laughs when you were in the army together. He called your Sergeant Dulcie Dubbin.

BOB: Old Pip – he'd come out with anything.

ROSEMARY: Do you like him at all?

BOB: Pip? I've known Pip for years.

ROSEMARY: I dunno – he seems funny to me.

[PIP *comes in with the coffee tray. Puts it down and takes the whiskey bottle from* ROSEMARY. *Speaks in a stage Irish accent*.]

PIP: A little drop of something to lift us all into Christmas Day.

[*He starts pouring whiskey, and cream over a spoon.*]

IRIS [*to* PIP]: Bob's thinking of taking a new place.

PIP: I hope not. [*Pouring cream*] I like it here best.

IRIS: Apparently he's fed up with S.E.16. He fancies a business more in the Thames Valley.

ROSEMARY: Or Marlow! Marlow's lovely.

IRIS [*to* PIP]: He thinks he'll get a better class of young customer up there. He fancies facilities for dancing.

ROSEMARY: And a grill. Charcoal grill's nice.

IRIS [*to* PIP]: And putting on dinners. With prawn cocktail. Rosemary's got all the ideas. Bob thinks she's got a sharp little nose for business.

PIP [*suddenly positive*]: I think it sounds revolting. Here you are, love. [*He hands her a cup.*]

BOB: What sounds revolting?

PIP: The Thames Valley. And the local Young Conservatives' annual do. Throwing bread rolls and gobbling down scampi and selections from *The Sound of Music* and Pimms No. 1 and stripping off in punts. [*He gives coffee to* ROSEMARY.] Coffee, love?

ROSEMARY [*angry*]: I'm not your love.

IRIS: And overdrafts and dud cheques and ten barmaids – all with eyelashes.

PIP: I don't think that's the sort of place I would want to visit. [*He gives coffee to* BOB.]

BOB [*puzzled*]: Thanks, Pip.

ROSEMARY: Well. No one's asking you.

[*Silence.* BOB *and* IRIS *are looking at* ROSEMARY. PIP *goes to the piano stool. Sits on it quite still.* ROSEMARY *repeats, with extra courage.*]

No one'll be asking you for Christmas. Not necessarily.

[BOB *moves over to* PIP *as if to protect him: but he doesn't say anything. He puts his coffee down on the piano.*]

PIP: No. I suppose they won't.

ROSEMARY: I mean, I'm not exactly sure. Are you the kids' uncle?

PIP: I'm just someone who comes for Christmas.

BOB [*protecting*]: You'll be welcome, Pip, wherever ...

ROSEMARY: Who is he? I'd like to know that first. Before we start extending invitations. [*Puts down her coffee and moves towards* PIP.]

BOB: He's an old family friend, that's who he is, Rosemary.

ROSEMARY: Yes, I can tell he's old.

BOB: This'll interest you. His Mum inhabits a castle.

ROSEMARY: Well, why don't he go to her for Christmas?

PIP: It's a question everyone seems to be asking.

BOB: Because he always stays with me.

ROSEMARY: Always?

BOB: That's what I said.

ROSEMARY: Why – is he your long lost cousin, or something?

BOB: He's no relation.

ROSEMARY: Then who is he?

IRIS [*to* PIP]: Why don't you tell her who you are?

[*But* PIP *ignores this. He looks at* BOB. *Lifts his hands to the piano and plays, singing.*]

BOB [*to* PIP]: Is that the one we're going to do?

PIP: We ought to start practising it.

BOB: How's it go?

PIP: The descant?

BOB: Yes. How's it go?

[PIP *plays the descant.* BOB *sings, looking at the sheet of music.*]

ROSEMARY: What's going on?

IRIS [*as* PIP *goes on playing, she puts down her coffee*]: It's a practice, Rosemary ... It's gone on since the three of us got to know each other. It started for ourselves, really; although now we do it for the children. Christmas Night when we never open – we sing them a carol. And Mr Lester, that's Pip, him being musical, he insists on a practice and a proper perform- ance. The kid's don't care much, quite frankly, but we enjoy it. [*She goes over to the piano, looks at the sheet of music. To* PIP] Which is my verse?

IRIS [*sings*]:

> The Holly bears a prickle
> As sharp as any thorn
> And Mary bore sweet Jesus Christ
> To be a Saviour.

ROSEMARY: I think it's bloody ridiculous!

PIP: Why? Bob's got a modest baritone and Iris might be described as a plucky soprano. It's not good, but it's not ridiculous.

ROSEMARY: I don't know why you don't open Christmas Day, and give a party, or have a dance or something for God's sake. Why just sit around singing hymns! I still don't know who he is. Anyway, I don't know why we need to have him every Christmas. [*To* BOB] You're not married to the man, are you?

[*Long pause.* IRIS *looks round.*]

IRIS: I think it's time someone told her.

PIP [*looks back at* IRIS]: Someone?

[*They both look at* BOB; *he takes a deep breath.*]

BOB: A long time ago. Eighteen years to be precise. Pip and I met as we was placed under the care of a maniac – Sergeant named by him 'Dulcie' – and we spent long, pointless days stamping on a dreary bit of parade ground near a dump called Bishop's Stortford. Well, one Christmas Eve a change came. Pip took me into his mother's house and played the piano in a high room with walls the colour of old birthday cake and we drank whiskey from a decanter while we got pissed bloody senseless. On the way home we climbed into a haystack that was all hard with frost, and we saw each other's breath in the moonlight. And suddenly, for no good reason, we grabbed each other like we were both drowning and proceeded to have it away as if all that side of life had just been invented. I regret to tell you, Rosemary, it didn't stop then. It's been going on ever since. So that's why Pip here's kept up with the family, and why he often brings the odd present at Christmas.

IRIS: Well, then. Now we all know.

[ROSEMARY *has been listening with growing incredulity. At*

the end of the speech, she looks at the three of them grouped, silent, dignified round the piano. Her hand covers her mouth as if she's not sure whether to break into a scream or giggles. Then she turns and runs away through the kitchen. We can hear the back door slam after her, when everything is quiet.]

IRIS: We do this bit together, don't we?
PIP: Oh, yes.

[PIP *plays. They all sing together.*]

> The Holly and the Ivy
> When they are both full grown
> Of all the trees that are in the wood
> The Holly bears the crown.
>
> The rising of the sun
> And the running of the deer.
> The playing of the merry organ,
> Sweet singing in the choir.

Curtain.

MARBLE ARCH

Marble Arch was first produced at the New Theatre, London, on 27 January 1970 with the following cast:

LAURA LOGAN	*Glynis Johns*
MCNEE	*Joss Ackland*
MISS PARKER	*Pauline Collins*
MAX	*Denholm Elliott*

Place: Laura Logan's flat in Marble Arch Mansions, W.2.

Time: Friday morning.

LAURA LOGAN's *flat near Marble Arch. Lots of wrought-iron furniture, white furry rugs, white leather chairs. Centre – the bedroom. A big double bed unmade, dressing table, etc., white TV. Door left leads to a bathroom and a lavatory. We can see a part of the bathroom floor and wall behind the shut door. Door right leads to a hall into which the flat's front door, and kitchen and sitting-room doors open. A tallboy in the hall beside a hall table.* LAURA LOGAN *– one-time toast of the Rank Organization, Queen of Pinewood and star of a dozen forgotten British movies – is on the bed, red hair and pearls in place, wearing a flowing black négligé and doing her slimming exercises. On a chair by the bed, a man's dark jacket, waistcoat and tie. By the bed, an opened bottle of champagne and two glasses, a tray with coffee and toast for two, half eaten. Around the flat, photographs of* LAURA *in low-cut dresses, riding habits, etc., signed pictures of James Mason, Stewart Granger, Patricia Roc and Margaret Lockwood. She stops exercising and shouts at the bathroom door.*

LAURA: Max! Max! [*She gets off the bed, pushes her feet into furry slippers.*] What's happened to you in there, Max? [*Shouts at the bathroom door*] Don't you have to be back downstairs by ten-thirty? Hurry up for heaven's sake! Your lady wife'll be back from bridge with her mother in Horsham, and all those sticky little drinks after dinner which stopped her driving back last night. [*She goes to the dressing table, starts brushing her hair.*] Do you realize if it hadn't been for the breathalyser, I'd never have the full glory of a whole night in bed with you once a week, Max? And your filthy pipe in my Charles of the Ritz cleansing cream! [*Doing her eyes*] For all these years – I only had you up to eleven-thirty Thursday evenings, and now – thanks to the inspiration of the Ministry of Transport, you can stay until Friday morning ... Big deal! Big, enormous, sumptuous deal ... [*She looks at the door curiously.*] Got a sudden attack of courage, or something? I mean, you're not going to run the risk of letting Phyllis find out, are you? [*Stops making *up, talks to the door.*] Did I tell you, Max – I met your little Phyllis in the lift last week? Really, I hardly noticed her against the beige of the wallpaper . . . and she said 'Saw your old movie on the telly last night, Miss Logan . . . Amazing to see those movies now,' she said. 'Isn't it, Miss Logan?' [*She gets up, goes to the bathroom, shouts at it.*] Come on, Max! For God's sake – are you going to spend all day in my loo, contemplating . . .? [*She moves back to the dressing table.*] I said, 'No doubt movies always struck you as bloody amazing, particularly the arrival of talkies which must have come as something of a shock to you – late in life' . . . Don't worry, I didn't say that really . . . I mean, we couldn't say that to little Phyllis, could we? Phyllis has to be taken care of . . . [*She stands up and crosses to the champagne. Picks up the bottle and shakes it, her hand over the top, to restore the fizz.*] And what do I get? Six nights a week on my own, watching television. [*She picks up a glass.*] The Golden Years of the British Cinema! You won't even take me out to dinner. Oh no! We can't be seen together! All the portions of Israeli Melon and Coq au Vin and stuff en croûte you never dared buy me in public. Well, at least I made you pay for them, Max! One thousand and fifty-three dinners at the Mirabelle in cash. In shoe boxes under my bed! [*She stoops and pulls out a cardboard shoe box, opens it, showing it's full of five-pound notes – gestures with it rudely at the door.*] Don't you think that's humiliating for me – having all my nights out in shoe boxes? You're a coward, Max! What's the good of you owning two film studios and thirty-three Orpheum Cinemas and Birmingham Week-end Television if you can't announce the take-over of a human person?

[*The phone rings beside the bed. She stuffs the shoe box back under it.*]

Who the hell's that?

[*She pours herself another glass of champagne, drinks, picks up the phone and answers it in a purring actress's telephone voice, gentler and more former Rank charm school than the tones in which she has been abusing Max.*]

Hullo? Yes. Yes, this is Miss Logan speaking . . . [*She covers the *mouthpiece and talks to the door*] It's the B.B.C., Max. That's not one of yours is it? [*Uncovers mouthpiece*] What? New Zealand Service? You want to what . . .? You mean they've just got around to seeing my films in New Zealand? Have they heard about the Battle of Alamein . . .? . . . Oh yes. Well, of course you can interview me. Be delighted. From ten-thirty this morning I'll be free until next Thursday evening. [*She puts down the phone, says gloomily*] It seems there's a good deal of interest in me, down under. [*She flops down on the bed drinking champagne.*] Interviews! It'll be quite like old times. I had a career once, remember? The day you first met me. Stage B at Shepperton, I was running down an iron staircase with nothing on but a few stuck-on sequins and an arse full of feathers. 'Mignonette . . . Folies Girl and Heroine of the Resistance.' Well . . . they really wanted Margaret Lockwood. They got her after that, didn't they, darling? After you snatched me out of the public gaze, and stuck me in the flat above you and Phyllis so you could just creep up in the lift on Thursdays! Swine Max! [*She sits down on the edge of the bed, shouts at the closed door*] If you'd ever had the decency to marry me . . . I'd bloody well divorce you. [*She gets up, puts the glass on the bedside table, and walks up and down, furious.*] What's in it for me . . .? Sweating it out up here on massage and Easy Slim Biscuits so I can always be little feather-tailed Mignonette when I want to be your wife with a coat and skirt from Debenham's Outsize Department and twin beds where we could lie reading until we fell quietly asleep, and didn't care who knew it. I'm fed up with all this secrecy! Who do you think you are, anyway? It's like having it off with the Pope or something. [*She stands in front of the bathroom door. Shouts at it*] I used to be young, Max. Can you hear me? I sat here on Monday, watching television. And there was I, a slip of a girl being raped by Stewart Granger, and I saw myself – all tear-stained with my lace jabot rudely torn away – and I said, 'Cheer up, darling . . . there's worse in store for you! Buried alive. That's what you're going to be. By the Chairman of the Board!' Max! Max! [*Enraged, she beats on the door.*] Why can't you answer? What's the matter with you? Have you dropped dead in there? [*She turns the handle and pushes the door violently. Greatly to her surprise, it is not locked. It opens. She goes into the bathroom and looks. She stands for a moment, looking in horror.*] Oh, Max ... you have! [*Then she returns to the bedroom, shutting the door reverently. Long pause.*] Max ... my poor Max. [*She goes to the bedside table, takes a cigarette out of a white alabaster box and lights it with her hand trembling. She sits down on the bed, facing the closed door, blowing out smoke. Long pause.*] What do you think people are going to say ...? [*Pause.*] I've got your reputation to think of. [*Pause.*] Oh, Max ... if you wanted to die, why couldn't you do it in your own flat?

[*There's a ring at the front doorbell.*]

Who's that?

[*The ring is repeated. She gets up slowly, looks despairingly at the bathroom door.*]

You'll get me thrown out of here, Max. Don't you know this place belongs to the Church Commissioners ...?

[*The ring comes again. She moves out of the bedroom to the hall.*]

They even fuss if you get too noisy playing the Epilogue. Who is it?

MCNEE: It's me, Miss Logan.

LAURA: Oh, McNee ...

[*She opens the door a crack. We can see a small segment of* MCNEE, *the porter, standing at the door. He has gold-rimmed glasses, a severe expression and a Scots accent.*]

MCNEE: I just brought up your things from the cleaner, Miss Logan.

LAURA: Thanks, McNee. I'll take it ... [*She opens the door a crack further, takes the cleaning, a couple of dresses on a hanger.*]

MCNEE: I'll be up in about five minutes for the rubbish, Miss Logan.

LAURA [*very nervous*]: I ... I haven't got any rubbish today, thank you very much. [*She goes into the bedroom, puts the cleaning on the bed.*]

MCNEE [*incredulous*]: No rubbish?

LAURA: No rubbish at all ... [*She shuts the bedroom door.*]

MCNEE: There must be rubbish in your tidy bin ... Miss Logan. [*He pushes the door open and goes towards the kitchen. From kitchen off*] I'll be back directly.

[LAURA, *who hasn't heard him, goes through the bedroom to the bathroom, turns away her head as she opens the bathroom door a crack, gets out the key from the inside of the door, and shuts the door again and locks it on the outside, leaving the key in the lock. She starts to move towards the telephone.*]

LAURA: Who do I ring ... Dr Fruteman? [*She sits on the bed, the telephone on her lap. Looks at it.*] Oh, Dr Fruteman ... I think there's a man dead in my loo ... [*She looks up at the bathroom door.*] Max ... How could you!

[*She starts to dial. As she does so,* MCNEE *comes out of the kitchen and crosses the hall.*]

[*To the phone*] Oh ... Is Dr Fruteman in, please? ... You expect him any moment? Could you ask him to give me a ring? It's Miss Logan ... Laura Logan. [*Annoyed*] No, I won't spell it! It used to be a household word. [*She puts down the phone.*] If only Dr Fruteman could find you passed away peacefully ... in your own bed, Max ... [*She puts the phone back on the bedside table. Moves towards the bathroom door and speaks at it*] Don't you see, darling ... it'd be so much more pleasant. [*She moves round the room.*] Well, it's only just downstairs ... you'd only have to go down one floor to it. There's a lift ... There's ... a ... [*An idea is dawning*] ... a lift! [*She goes to the door and speaks to it quickly, persuasively*] It's just one floor, Max! But it'd make all the difference. All right? [*No answer, so she answers herself.*] All right ... [*She moves quickly to the telephone.*] I'll need help, that's all. [*She looks at the telephone and then starts to dial.*] Is that Harrods? Oh, could you give me your Removal Department please? Removals. You undertake all sorts of removals? I don't mean of anything ... I mean of anybody. Alive or dead ... Well, I'm trying to explain. It's simply a question ...

[*Front door bell rings.*]

Oh ... I'll call you back. [*She slams down the telephone.*] It's
always the same! Mend my own fuses – fix my own drinks ...
[*Speaks to the bathroom door*] See what it's like, Max – being
a woman on your own?

[*She goes through the bedroom door quickly, and shuts it behind
her. She takes a deep breath, and opens the front door slowly.
MCNEE is standing there, with a rubbish disposal trolley. Two
wheels and a long handle to which is fitted a large sack of
reinforced paper, held open by a large circle of iron at the top
and with a metal cover.*]

MCNEE: Bring out your dead, Miss Logan!
LAURA: What?

[*She moves back appalled as he walks past her. He stops to open
the kitchen door. The rubbish disposal trolley between them.*]

MCNEE: It's my wee joke, Miss Logan. Something I often say,
when I'm collecting the rubbish.
LAURA: Very ... funny!
MCNEE: Sorry to keep ringing. I left my pass key downstairs.
LAURA: That's all right.
MCNEE: Not disturbing you, I hope ...?
LAURA: Oh, not at all really. [*As he gets the trolley*] You've got
a pass key, have you ...?
MCNEE: Downstairs ...
LAURA: So you can get into any of the flats ...?
MCNEE: Oh yes. I have to. In case of accident ...
LAURA: In case of accident! [*She looks at him hard.*] Mr McNee
... You know the flat below here?
MCNEE: Number 4?
LAURA: Yes. Number 4 ... Is the lady from Number 4 ... back
yet?
MCNEE: I don't think so. The car's not outside.
LAURA: I was just wondering ...
MCNEE: Well, I'll just trundle this wee dustbin into your kitchen.
LAURA [*looks at the dustbin, fingers it thoughtfully*]: It's not so
wee, is it? ...

MCNEE: What's not so wee?

LAURA: Your dustbin . . .?

MCNEE: No . . .

LAURA: No. In fact, it's quite large. [*She opens the lid and looks into it.*] And empty.

MCNEE: I made you my first call . . .

LAURA: You could get . . . quite a lot of rubbish in there.

MCNEE: It's surprising.

LAURA: Strong, is it?

MCNEE: Double thickness, wet-reinforced, ten-ply wood-pulp paper, you'd be surprised the objects it's had in it . . .

LAURA: Would I . . .?

MCNEE: As I often say, you can know a tenant by his rubbish . . .

LAURA: I suppose you can. Mr McNee. [*She grips his wrist.*]

MCNEE: Yes, Miss Logan?

LAURA: Please . . . [*She starts to pull him towards the bedroom door.*] Just come with me for a moment.

MCNEE: I've no got the time . . . The regulation is – all rubbish out of sight by ten-fifteen a.m.

LAURA: He's strict, isn't he?

MCNEE: Who?

LAURA: Our landlord. Who is it – the Archbishop of Canterbury? [*She has got to the bedroom door – opens it.*]

MCNEE [*as she gets him into the bedroom*]: I'm told his Grace does keep a wee personal eye on the property.

LAURA [*she goes to the champagne bottle, shakes it to bring up the fizz*]: And Marble Arch Mansions – was never touched by a breath of scandal.

MCNEE: Our reputation's untarnished.

LAURA: No suicides . . . no divorces. [*She pours out a glass of champagne for* MCNEE.] Have a drink . . . And no pets!

MCNEE: Not during the hours of duty. Pets are not allowed.

LAURA [*advancing on him with the glass*]: But all the same, they're here, aren't they?

[*During the following dialogue she comes nearer and nearer to him, threateningly.*]

MCNEE: What's here?

LAURA: Pets!

MCNEE: Pets? [*Shakes his head.*] Never! All animals forbidden, Miss Logan. [*He retreats from her, defensive.*]

LAURA: Only in theory, isn't that so?

MCNEE: It's my personal responsibility ...

LAURA: In the night-time, I hear poodles coughing.

MCNEE: ... to see there are no animals on the premises ...

LAURA: I've seen turtles going up in the service lift ...

MCNEE: Well, you have to turn a blind eye occasionally!

LAURA: Exactly! [*She pushes the glass into his hand.*] And how much does Mrs Montefiore pay you to keep quiet about her miniature Peruvian apes?

MCNEE [*takes a quick drink from the glass of flat champagne*]: It would be more than my job's worth.

LAURA: And what about the Guildersleeves in 6A?

MCNEE: What about them ...?

LAURA: If they're married, my name's Anna Neagle!

MCNEE: Some things are better taken at their face value, Miss Logan ...

LAURA: And the two stockbrokers in Number 7!

MCNEE: Flatmates – from the landlord's point of view ...

LAURA: And the sweet smell of Miss Cantor's cigarette is rare Egyptian tobacco, and those two married couples go into Number 9 every evening in full riding habit to play bridge.

MCNEE: You have to paper over the cracks once in a while, Miss Logan ...

LAURA: Then paper over this one!

MCNEE: Which one?

LAURA: There's somebody dead in my bathroom.

MCNEE [*quickly empties his glass*]: Somebody ...?

LAURA [*moves to the bed, gets the bottle of champagne*]: Dead.

MCNEE [*looks at her disapprovingly*]: Oo ... Miss Logan, you haven't ...?

LAURA [*fills his glass*]: Natural causes.

MCNEE: Is it someone you know?

LAURA: You know him too.

MCNEE: Who ...?

LAURA: The gentleman from Number 4.

MCNEE: But he's ... a public figure ...

LAURA: He has his private moments.

MCNEE [*lowers his voice*]: You say he's passed over ...?

LAURA [*looks at the bathroom door, she speaks in a lowered voice also*]: Yes.

MCNEE: In there ...?

LAURA: Yes.

MCNEE: But surely he's got a bathroom of his own ...?

LAURA: No doubt.

MCNEE: So what on earth ...?

LAURA [*suddenly aloud*]: Oh, for heaven's sake, Mr McNee. You don't think he came up here just because he felt like snuffing out, do you?

MCNEE [*thoughtful*]: No ... I suppose he no did that ...

LAURA: Life Peers don't seek this place out to die – like elephants!

MCNEE: Oo ... Miss Logan. The landlords're no going to care for this ...

LAURA: The landlords're no going to know.

MCNEE: It'll be in the papers ...

LAURA: That he passed away in his own bed, while his wife was visiting her mother, and was found by their cleaning lady shortly before ... eleven. That's when she arrives, isn't it?

MCNEE: What're you suggesting?

LAURA: Simply do your job, Mr McNee.

MCNEE: What job?

LAURA: Have the rubbish taken down. By ten-fifteen.

MCNEE: That's no a very nice way to refer to the gentleman.

LAURA: But that's what he is, at the moment. Don't you understand, Mr McNee? When you've taken him down to where he belongs, he'll be highly respected again. He'll be a force for good in the British Cinema, and the only Labour Peer to sell coloured television sets to Albania. And to me he'll be ... well, he'll be how I always knew him. But at the moment – he's disposable.

MCNEE: I can't do it, Miss Logan.

LAURA: Are these service flats or aren't they?

MCNEE: Certain basic services – are provided.

LAURA: What could be more basic than this?

MCNEE: The Church Commissioners would nay like it ...

LAURA: 'Lord Hammersmith found dead in wrong bathroom in

Marble Arch Mansions' splashed all over the *Daily Sketch*. How's that going to tickle the Church Commissioners?

MCNEE [*doubtful*]: We've always done our best, Miss Logan, to make you comfortable at the Mansions ...

LAURA: Did I ever give you a Christmas Box? I rather ...

MCNEE: I'm sure ...

LAURA: I'm sure I forgot. Here ... [*She moves quickly to the bed, feels under it and pulls the cardboard shoe box. She takes out a handful of money.*]

[MCNEE *looks at it, fascinated.*]

Have some – of my dinner money!

MCNEE [*holds out his hand, taking the money*]: I'm not sure ... you didney forget Christmas ...

LAURA: And your birthday! [*She puts more money into his hand.*]

MCNEE: Down the service lift? It might be possible ...

[*He holds out his hand for more money.*
She puts the lid on the shoe box and puts it on the bed.]

LAURA: Final instalment – when the place is all tidy.

MCNEE: It'd be a comfort. To the poor widow.

LAURA: To us all ...

MCNEE [*moves towards the bed*]: I'll do it for you, Miss Logan.

LAURA: I'm sure you will. [*Moving between him and the shoe box. She puts the shoe box quickly under the dress from the cleaner's.*]

MCNEE: I'll just slip down and get the pass key ...

LAURA: Don't forget we haven't much time!

[*He goes quickly out of the bedroom and into the hall. He opens the front door of the flat and goes out hurriedly, failing to shut the door properly, so that it remains ajar.* LAURA *finds another cigarette, lights it. The telephone by the bed rings. At the same time the front door bell rings. She doesn't hear it. She picks up the telephone.*]

Yes ... Yes, this is Miss Logan speaking. Oh, Dr Fruteman ... how good of you to ring me back ...

[*The front door is pushed open. A girl in a long footballer's scarf, wearing a duffle coat and carrying a tape recorder on a strap over her shoulder, comes in and looks round and curiously at the dustbin.*]

MISS PARKER: Hello, Miss Logan ...

LAURA: Goodbye, Dr Fruteman.

MISS PARKER: I rang you from Bush House. Now, all ready for our little chinwag!

LAURA: Chinwag. I'm afraid that's out of the question now.

MISS PARKER: I'm thrilled to bits to meet you, Miss Logan. Is this your boudoir? Lovely. Listen, I wanted to take up the acting line myself. As a matter of fact I was singled out for praise by the *Auckland Star* for my Mr Rochester in the *Jane Eyre* of Charlotte Brontë. But when they ask me what I've done, and I say Mr Rochester at Auckland High, it doesn't help much towards getting those female roles I long for. Now, where shall we go?

LAURA: Nowhere!

MISS PARKER: Well, I had to come to London after all I'd heard about the sweet life in Earls Court, so I just bummed my way half round the world. It makes a fascinating story if you've got a moment.

LAURA: I haven't. Not a moment. I've got the workmen coming in. I'm having the place done over.

MISS PARKER: But you clearly said on the phone this morning ...

LAURA: That was another lifetime.

MISS PARKER: Are you aware someone's left a dustbin deposited in your lobby?

LAURA: Yes. Well ... how ridiculous.

MISS PARKER: It does create a somewhat ratty impression.

LAURA: That shouldn't be there.

MISS PARKER: Want me to move it for you?

LAURA: No ... No, I'll just put it in the kitchen ...

[MISS PARKER *switches on her tape recorder and speaks into it.*]

MISS PARKER: One-two-three-testing. [*Deep voice*] I love you, Jane. Jane ... We are free my darling ... [*To tape recorder*] My poor wife just burned to death in the west wing ... [*She puts down the microphone on the hall table by the tape recorder.*]

[LAURA *comes out of the kitchen into the hall.*]

LAURA: Miss Parker.

MISS PARKER: That looks better, doesn't it ...?

LAURA: Look ... Miss Parker ...

MISS PARKER: I never get round to tidying my own place this early either. Every morning my flat mate and I swear to God we'll get things shipshape before we go to work, but can we ever ...?

[*While* MISS PARKER *and* LAURA *are speaking* MAX *crosses the strip of tiled floor and tries the bathroom door. He is a large man who looks stunned, having momentarily passed out on the loo. He's wearing a shirt with a wing collar only attached by a black collar stud and striped trousers with the braces hanging down. He tries the lock. Finding it locked and hearing* MISS PARKER'*s voice from the hall, he retreats again out of sight. At the same time* LAURA *has got hold of* MISS PARKER *and starts to push her out of the flat.*]

LAURA: I'll have to ask you to go, Miss Parker, the fact is, I'm not feeling well ...

MISS PARKER [*speaking at the same time*]: Too bad ... you're feeling crook?

LAURA: The doctor's on his way up now, to give me a thorough check up. [*She is opening the front door.*]

MISS PARKER: Well, if you're not a hundred per cent ...

LAURA: I'm not. [*She has got* MISS PARKER *through the door and out into the corridor.*] Do ring me again. [*She starts to close the door on her.*] Fix up another appointment.

[*She has the door closed. She leans on it for a moment, gives a sigh of relief and goes into the bedroom, picks up the champagne bottle, shakes it to make it bubble, pours out a quick glass and looks at the clock.* MCNEE *opens the front door of the flat with his pass key. Comes in, his pass key on a big ring in his hand and looks for the trolley which he left in the hallway. Can't find it.* LAURA *goes to the bathroom door: turns the key*

[*so that* MCNEE *can remove* MAX. *As* MCNEE *reaches the bedroom door, there is a violent ring at the front door of the flat.* MCNEE *looks at it, guilty and alarmed, not wanting to be found there on his curious errand. He opens the kitchen door and goes quickly into it, shutting it behind him.* LAURA *crosses the bedroom to answer the front door. She comes into the hall and shuts the bedroom door behind her. She opens the front door;* MISS PARKER *is standing there.*]

I thought I told you . . .

MISS PARKER: Steady on, Miss Logan. I left my infernal machine!

[MAX *appears again in the bathroom, still dazed and vaguely hooking up his braces. He tries the bathroom door again, finds it unlocked and emerges into the bedroom. He leaves the bathroom door open, puts on his coat and waistcoat, but leaves his collar undone and forgets his tie. Then he tiptoes with elaborate caution to the bedroom door, is halted by the sound of voices still continuing and he stands with his hand on the bedroom door handle, his ear against the door listening.* MISS PARKER *starts to pack her tape recorder.*]

They'd've slaughtered me back at Bush House if I'd left this behind. Anyway, I'll need it for my next assignment. At this very address as it happens . . . I'm interviewing a tycoon of considerable note . . .

[*Both* LAURA *and* MAX *react to this.*]

LAURA: A what?

MISS PARKER: Lord Hammersmith in person. I was booked for a chinwag with him and I thought as you lived in the same building and you still being such a name in Auckland . . .

LAURA [*appalled*]: You're going down to Number 4 . . .?

MISS PARKER: Right now.

LAURA: You can't do that . . .

MISS PARKER: Why not . . .?

LAURA: Because . . . Because he won't speak to you . . .

MISS PARKER: Is he all that reserved?

LAURA: I've heard he's a very quiet man. Almost, totally silent.

MISS PARKER [*disappointed*]: And I was hoping for a few tough words from him on the sterling position – for the Dominions.

[*The kitchen door behind* MISS PARKER's *head slowly opens, and* MCNEE *peers out. He gestures to* LAURA *pointing at his wrist watch. She nods and grabs* MISS PARKER *by the wrist, and drags her towards the sitting-room door. At the same time* MCNEE *closes the kitchen door.*]

MISS PARKER: What was that?

LAURA: Just my cleaning lady. [*She takes her arm.*] Come in here with me. I'll give the Dominions something better than the sterling position.

MISS PARKER: Honest, Miss Logan?

LAURA: In the sitting-room. That suit you?

MISS PARKER: Too right! I promise you it'll be much appreciated.

LAURA [*opening the sitting-room door*]: We won't be disturbed in here . . .

[*As* LAURA *is moving* MISS PARKER *towards the sitting-room door which they are both facing,* MAX *opens the bedroom door a crack and peers out. Alarmed at seeing a strange woman in the flat, he retreats into the bedroom quickly. As he does so,* LAURA *gets* MISS PARKER *into the sitting-room.*]

MISS PARKER [*on her way into the sitting-room*]: How long can you give me, Miss Logan?

LAURA: Oh, just as long as it takes . . .

[*The sitting-room door shuts on them. This happens just at the same moment as* MAX *has shut the bedroom door. At the same moment,* MCNEE *opens the kitchen door and comes out. He looks round the hall, makes sure the coast is clear and goes back into the kitchen to fetch his trolley.* MAX *opens the door a little, sees the trolley being moved towards the bedroom and then moves back and hides behind the bedroom door just as* MCNEE *opens it, and tramps straight through the bedroom, into the bathroom with his trolley. As soon as* MCNEE *is in the bathroom,* MAX *whips out of the bedroom and into the hall. He looks into the hall mirror and sees his tie is missing – starts to go back*] *into the bedroom when the sitting-room door opens.* MAX *moves to hide behind the tallboy in the hall. At the same time* MCNEE *moves, looking puzzled, into the visible part of the bathroom.*]

MISS PARKER [*off*]: Miss Logan, if you don't mind, I'll just get some of your pearls of memory down on tape. Half a mo …

[MISS PARKER *comes quickly out of the sitting-room, grabs the tape recorder from the hall table, and is back again as* LAURA *appears at the sitting-room door. In the bathroom* MCNEE *is scratching his head.*]

LAURA: Come back here …!
MISS PARKER: All set, Miss Logan!
LAURA: All right!

[MISS PARKER *goes into the sitting-room.* LAURA *shuts the sitting-room door on both of them. In the bathroom* MCNEE *shrugs his shoulders and starts to move his empty trolley out.* MAX *is emerging from behind the tallboy in the hall when* MCNEE *bangs the bathroom door shut behind him. At this moment* MAX *quickly opens the kitchen door and goes into the kitchen.* MCNEE *walks straight through the bedroom into the hall with his trolley. As he passes the sitting-room door,* MCNEE *knocks on it and calls out.*]

MCNEE: Your bathroom's all clear as far as I can see, Miss Logan.
LAURA [*calls from the sitting-room off*]: Thank you, Mr McNee … I'll speak to you later.
MCNEE: I'll be back directly …

[MCNEE *pushes his trolley out of the front door and bangs the door of the flat shut.* MAX *then opens the kitchen door and comes out into the hall. He hurries back into the bedroom to get his tie, sees it hanging on the chair and starts to put it on, leaving the bedroom door open. The sitting-room door opens and* LAURA *comes out, she looks round nervously.* MISS PARKER *comes out after her, her tape recorder slung round her shoulder, holding out the microphone to catch* LAURA'S *every word.*]

LAURA: I'm sorry. My memory's rather short this morning. They'll have to make do with that.

MISS PARKER: I was hoping you might have a little more for your old fans, Miss Logan.

[*The bedroom door is open.* MAX *retreats at the sound of* MISS PARKER's *voice towards the bathroom.* LAURA *moves away from* MISS PARKER *towards the bedroom door.*]

LAURA: Excuse me.

[*As* LAURA *goes to the bedroom,* MAX *quietly shuts the bathroom door. He stands on the strip of tiled floor as* LAURA *comes into the bedroom followed by* MISS PARKER.]

MISS PARKER: Perhaps we could get a bit further than your one trip to Hollywood.

LAURA [*looks round the room*]: Forgive me! It's been a morning ... [*She sits down, tired, on the edge of the bed.*]

[MISS PARKER *comes close up to her, holding the microphone.* MAX *puts his hand in his pocket, finds his pipe, takes it out and while he is waiting fills it from a tobacco pouch, sticks it in his mouth and finds a box of matches.*]

MISS PARKER: I'd like a scrap or two on the purely personal level. If you feel up to it.

LAURA: On the personal level?

MISS PARKER: Your name's never been coupled with any romantic attachment?

LAURA: Is that of any interest, to my fans down under?

[*In the bathroom* MAX *has got his pipe lit. He moves out of sight to throw the match down the loo.*]

MISS PARKER: Why, stone the crows, Miss Logan, I'd say of absorbing interest. Was there any particular male at all concerned.

LAURA: Any particular male?

[*In the bathroom* MAX *returns to view, blowing out smoke.*]

MISS PARKER: That made any deep impression on you?

LAURA: There was, now you ask me, one lasting relationship ...

[MISS PARKER *kneels on the floor and holds the microphone out to* LAURA.]

MISS PARKER: Could you say it again, a little closer to the mike?

LAURA: I am issuing this statement to you, Miss Parker, on the strict understanding it goes no further than the other side of the world . . .

MISS PARKER: You were married once . . .?

LAURA: Only on Thursdays.

[MAX *waits, anxious at what she is going to give away.*]

MISS PARKER: What? [*She holds the microphone closer to* LAURA.]

LAURA: He only had time for me once a week, although I had time for him always. But on a Thursday, when his family was otherwise occupied in Horsham, he would slip up here and make what can only be described as love . . . [*She pauses.*]

[*Still with his pipe in his mouth* MAX *stoops down and listens, his ear to the keyhole, concerned, but also flattered at what he only half understands.*]

MISS PARKER: Carry on, Miss Logan.

LAURA: He was the kindest man – and the most considerate lover. Love with him was like being handed gracefully into the warm, carpeted inside of a Daimler Hire. Our life together was not what might be considered exciting nowadays. I'd cook him roast lamb and rice pudding. His favourite programme was 'Come Dancing' and, more often than not, we'd be in bed before ten o'clock. But when we got there, it was extremely relaxed. There was a small vein in his forehead that pounded away when he read the *Financial Times*, and when I saw his head against the ribbons of my nightdress, that vein was quite still. He was an extremely clean man whose hands smelt of Wright's Coal Tar Soap.

MISS PARKER: He sounds an almost perfect person . . .

LAURA: He had his weaknesses. Collecting – all manner of things. Old envelopes, bits of string, cotton reels, worn out rubber bands. He'd smooth out used brown paper and put it aside and say, 'When the market falls this'll line my shoes on a wet evening'. He wouldn't go near the Embankment, on which he thought he'd end up sleeping.

MISS PARKER: What's happened to him now, Miss Logan?

LAURA: He's passed over.

[MAX *is listening in extreme astonishment, takes out his pipe.*]

MISS PARKER: Recently?

LAURA: It seems – some time ago now. Of course, I attended the funeral ...

[MAX *puts his still lit pipe into his jacket pocket as he hears this.*]

MISS PARKER: Naturally ...

LAURA: Incognito. Being neither family nor business, I sat between his numerous relatives and innumerable employees like a stranger. I refused, with dignity, the invitation to attend the large chicken dinner with which his departure was celebrated.

MISS PARKER: My oath! It must have been a most moving occasion ...

LAURA: It was as he wanted it ...

[MAX's *pipe has begun to burn his jacket pocket and the clouds of smoke are increasing rapidly.*]

LAURA: No fuss and no flowers. Simply the band of the Salvation Army playing selections from Rodgers and Hammerstein ...

[MCNEE *opens the front door with his pass key and comes into the hall, where he is stopped by the sound of voices from the bedroom.*]

The Prime Minister was represented, and the urn was put where we always planned, with a view out all over Golders Green.

[*Suddenly* MAX *notices that he is on fire and starts to slap wildly at his pocket to put himself out.*]

I hope he's happy where he is now. He always had a strong fear of foreign travel.

[LAURA *and* MISS PARKER *are silent. The front door opens,* MCNEE *comes into the hall.*
MAX, *who has failed to put himself out, moves further into the bathroom out of our view, to get water.*]

MCNEE: Miss Logan ...

[*Still wrapped in her golden memories of Max,* LAURA *doesn't answer him.*

MCNEE *knocks on the bedroom door. The sound of his knock is drowned by the sudden rush of a tap and various crashes from the bathroom.* MAX *backs into our view in the bathroom again, sloshing water from a tooth mug over his coat.*

At the same moment, MCNEE *opens the bedroom door – sees* LAURA.]

MCNEE: Miss Logan, I came to report to you that . . . [*Sees* MISS PARKER.]

LAURA [*looking amazed at the bathroom door.*]: Whatever . . .

[*She turns and crosses the bedroom to pull open the bathroom door.* MISS PARKER, *her tape machine slung around her, has risen to her feet and* MCNEE *is following* LAURA *to the bathroom door of which they both have a full view as* LAURA *pulls it open to reveal the soaked and extinguished* MAX. MAX *turns and smiles at them with a look of perfect calm and self-confidence.*]

LAURA: Max!

MISS PARKER: Don't I recognize these famous features?

MCNEE: My lord! You are in the bathroom . . .

MAX: Good morning, McNee. 'Morning everyone.

MISS PARKER: Gee whiz. You wouldn't read about it. Is his lordship often to be found among your toilet facilities?

LAURA [*still amazed*]: No . . .

MAX: No, of course not. I just popped up actually . . .

LAURA: You're alive . . .!

MAX: Alive? Of course I'm alive. It's not all that dangerous, you know. Fixing the plumbing. Gets you a bit on the wettish side, of course . . .

LAURA: Fixing the what?

MAX: I tell you, McNee, last night I hardly slept a wink! I was kept awake by the pipes up here gargling like the Hallelujah Chorus! So this morning, tired out and exhausted, I called up and asked if I might personally inspect my neighbour's ball-cock. It was pretty gruelling work, I might say actually. [*Starts to pull a gold watch out of his waistcoat pocket. Then speaks to*

LAURA *with meaning*.] I must've snoozed off in there for forty winks. Didn't want to burst in when you had visitors . . . [*Looks at his watch*.] Good heavens! Is that the time? I must be trotting along. [*He moves towards the door.* MISS PARKER *is trotting after him like a small terrier*.] I don't think you'll have any more trouble with your pipes.

MISS PARKER [*running after* MAX]: Lord Hammersmith, Oh Hoo Roo, Miss Logan. Lord Hammersmith! My Lord, what do you think of the sterling position?

MAX: The sterling position? What position is that, my dear? [*He pats her bottom jovially as they go out of the door together*.]

[MAX *and* MISS PARKER *are out through the front door.* LAURA *is standing in the centre of the bedroom. Then she picks the dress up, to put it away, reveals the shoe box.* MCNEE *looks at it, she looks at him*.]

MCNEE: There you are, Miss Logan, things are n'ere so bad as they are painted. There's no need to explain, Miss Logan. We must just see that the landlord's asked no awkward questions.

[LAURA *gives* MCNEE £*10*.]

Thank you, Miss Logan. I'll be up again tomorrow morning for your rubbish. As I often say – you can tell a tenant by her rubbish.

[LAURA *doesn't answer. He goes.*
LAURA *is alone on the stage. She starts listlessly to tidy up. Then she stops and sits on the bed. Slumped inert. She gets out a cigarette, lights it. Then immediately stubs it out in the bedside ashtray as the phone rings. She is on her feet, eyes blazing, angry*.]

LAURA: Max! Where the hell are you phoning from? Your kitchen. Where's Phyllis – not back? And Miss Down Under, oh she's in the lounge, is she . . . Listen to me – you're a coward, Max! A complete total one hundred per cent, terrified coward. You couldn't even die up here, could you? That's what I've got – a place you wouldn't be seen dead in. Wha . . . What're you talking about? Of course I'm not the Board of Trade. Oh, Phyllis has just walked in the room, has she? Well, why don't you tell her, Max? Why not ...? You think I'm going to stay up here ... like a prisoner ... always? Oh ... Oh Phyllis slipped out to the shops. What ... what did you say? Oh, I suppose so ... [*The anger goes out of her suddenly*.] All right, then. Yes, I'll be here ... See you, Max. Thursday as usual. See you ... lover.

[*She puts the phone down slowly. She picks up the stubbed-out cigarette, relights it with her lighter – sighs and goes slowly back to the routine of her everyday life. She goes into the bathroom.* SOUND *of water as she turns on the bath.*]

The curtain falls.

THE FEAR OF HEAVEN

The Fear of Heaven was first presented at the Greenwich Theatre on 28 May 1976 with the following cast:

LEWIS LUBY	*Denholm Elliott*
TOMMY FLETCHER	*Peter Woodthorpe*
SOPHIE LUBY	*Hana-Maria Pravda*
AN ENGLISH-SPEAKING GUIDE	*Alan Dudley*
A NUN	*Rita Giovannini*
A DOCTOR	*Trevor Baxter*
A YOUNG ITALIAN PATIENT	*Leonardo Pieroni*

The play directed by John Tydeman
Setting by Peter Rice

Scene: The action takes place in a ward of the Hospital for Transients and the Urban Poor, housed in the ancient Palazzo Martedi in a town in Tuscany.

Time: The present.

A ward of the Hospital for Transients and the Urban Poor, housed in the ancient Palazzo Martedi in a town in Tuscany. On the ceiling of the ward there is an important painting 'The Fear of Heaven', by Bernadino di Taddeo, names Il Zoppo, painted in the year 1453. At first the stage is in darkness, then a section of the ceiling is lit brilliantly but we see only a corner of the great picture of Heaven – an impression of a blue sky, floating clouds, green grass and a huge foot in a sandal with the big toe especially prominent – the big toe of God.

[*The* GUIDE *comes up from the audience, waving a walking-stick. He is a seedy man with a slight limp, in a black alpaca jacket stained with spaghetti and cigarette ash. He wears shapeless grey trousers.*]

GUIDE: This way, my group! English spoken! English spoken here! Eyes up, everyone! Upwards. That's what we've come to see. Heaven! 'The Fear of Heaven'.

[*It is now possible to see dimly the hospital beds upstage. In the centre two beds are hidden by green screens, from one of which comes the sound of oxygen breathing. In an unscreened bed L, a* YOUNG ITALIAN *is moaning and cursing quietly. A nursing* NUN *in a white habit enters and goes behind the screen.*]

The fear. That is to say, the awe. You might translate it the 'Wonder of Heaven'. [*He moves to another position.*] We are now directly beneath the feet of God the Father. This is the largest painting of a foot in Italy. God's big toe alone measures over three foot in length. Jolly impressive, isn't it?

[*The* NUN *comes out from behind the screen. The* YOUNG ITALIAN *shouts at her.*]

ITALIAN PATIENT: *Santa Maria! Un orinale.*

[*The* NUN *goes off, clucking disapproval.*
The GUIDE *is pointing at another part of the ceiling.*]

GUIDE: Just look up there on the lawn. Saints and philosophers, no doubt, having some jolly interesting conversations. Please notice the smiles on all those who have passed through the blessed gates.

[*The* NUN *returns with a glass bottle. With relief the* YOUNG ITALIAN *puts it under the bedclothes.*]

In Il Zoppo's beautiful painting of Heaven there are fifty-three varieties of wild flowers, all to be found in the hills of his native Tuscany. There are no fewer than thirty-one varieties of ornamental and singing birds. Quite a zoo, actually. [*He moves and points to another area of the ceiling.*]

[*The* NUN *leaves with the bottle.*]

In this corner the angels are playing sacred music on their instruments. Notice that they have the faces of good mature women and mothers of families. They are not irresponsible teenagers like the angels of Sandro Botticelli.

[*The* NUN *returns with a clipboard; and with* DOCTOR BENJAMINI, *a young Italian of great culture and charm, with horn-rimmed glasses, a white coat and a manner of bored indifference to the patients.*
The GUIDE *points upwards at a corner of the stage.*]

Over the door please notice the portrait of the Duke Alfonso de Martedi, who built this palace in the year thirteen hundred and ninety-two.

[*The* NUN *and* DOCTOR *have pushed the screens aside, making a square in the centre of the stage, in which the two central beds stand and we can see their unconscious occupants, their heads propped up by pillows. From where they lie they can only see upwards to the ceiling, the rest of the ward is screened off from their view. They are both English. One is* TOMMY FLETCHER, *short, broad, middle-aged, with a small moustache. He is lying breathing irregularly. The oxygen cylinder is standing, unused at the moment, beside his bed. In the next bed, also unconscious, is* LEWIS LUBY, *also middle-aged, a lecturer for the British Council. Both men are wearing striped flannel pyjamas. The* DOCTOR *feels* FLETCHER's *pulse in an uninterested way.*]

The whole building is now in use by the Government of Italy as a hospital for Transients and the Urban Poor.

[*The* DOCTOR *lets* FLETCHER's *wrist drop and moves downstage. The* NUN *goes and sits down on her chair.*]

You may now admire the ceiling for a few moments of leisure. Please be careful of the hospital equipment.

[*The* GUIDE *goes to the* DOCTOR *and offers him a cigarette from a battered packet.*]

Coffin peg, Doctor?

DOCTOR: *Grazie, tanto.* How are your tourists, keen?

[*The* DOCTOR *lights their cigarettes with a gold lighter. The* GUIDE *coughs into the smoke.*]

GUIDE: They will take their eyes off the ceiling and start peering at the patients.

DOCTOR: True, the patients are a great distraction. I often feel, with you, they spoil the beauty of this remarkable hospital. Today they brought us a couple more, English. You were not at the meeting of the English-Speaking Union at the Palazzo Publico?

GUIDE [*still coughing*]: Bit of jealousy there. I don't get asked.

DOCTOR: Just as well; the balcony collapsed.

GUIDE: I heard a sort of distant boom as we were doing the Martedi tombs. [*Coughing*] Well, I suppose we all end up here eventually.

DOCTOR: In this country we spend far too much trying to patch up our old people and too little, in my opinion, on preserving great works of art. Your visiting lecturer Signor Luby can take comfort. He fell from a balcony attributed to the great Palladio. It's a pleasure to have a man of culture here. Too often they lie with their eyes closed, listening to their radios. [*With disgust*] They only interest themselves in bed-pans and bottles of medicine. They never raise their eyes to the Great Work of Art above them.

GUIDE: Never?

DOCTOR: When they are dead, of course. Only when they are dead. We notice that the eyes are always directed upwards.

[*The* DOCTOR *stubs out his cigarette and goes.*
The GUIDE *squeezes his cigarette out and puts the stub in his breast pocket for later use. He returns to address his tourists.*]

GUIDE: All right, my group. Off to the Cathedral. Treats in store are Giotto's portrait of Santa Catherina and a small quantity of her liquefied blood. This way, please. Come along, all my English-speaking group.

[*The* GUIDE *goes.*
Silence. The NUN *starts to knit. The light changes as time passes.*]

YOUNG ITALIAN [*calling from his bed*]: Un orinale – per amor di Dio!
NUN [*sharply*]: Silencio! Tutti dormano.

[*The* YOUNG ITALIAN *switches on a transistor radio at the side of his bed. A short burst of Puccini's* Madam Butterfly.]

[*more sharply*]: Silencio! Il radio! L'Inglese e molto ammalato!

[*The* YOUNG ITALIAN *clicks off the radio. Silence. Then the sound of a clock chiming the quarters – it is about to strike the hour. Light increases on the ceiling which (by an increase of light on it or by a mechanical movement) seems to become larger and more dominant over the centre of the stage. At the same time the centre square between the screens becomes lighter and the rest of the ward more shadowy. Mr* LUBY *starts to stir and speaks.*]

LUBY: For the poet, madame – incest isn't a crime. It's a necessity!

[*The clock strikes – one.*]

What? What's that . . .? That bell? Where am I? *Where?* [*He feels for his glasses at the side of the bed, puts them on and looks up at the ceiling – then he sits up, panic stricken.*] No! Not *here!* It's impossible. Quite impossible. [*Appalled*] Oh, my God! You exist . . . ! [*Pause; he suddenly shouts*] This is Luby here! Lewis Luby! Atheist and man of letters! I have rejected you

– *completely*! I mean, even – even if ... You have defied the laws of probability. And of science ... You won't want me here, I'm sure. There's been a mistake ... A serious mistake. [*Louder*] A mistake! Can you hear me? [*Deeply worried*] Angels. Actually angels. Playing harps! This is quite absurd. It's high time I said – something outrageous. Wipe that serene look off their faces. [*He gets out of bed and calls up at the ceiling.*] You! You over there! *Madame. Signora. Senora. Liebe Frau!* My name is Luby and I am quite unable to find the slightest evidence of life after death. Did you hear that, all of you? I have never for one moment believed in the immortality of the soul! Let alone, let alone – this place! Well, you don't think the mere fact of being dead's going to change my mind, do you? I tell you, Lewis Luby's not so easily persuaded! You know my opinions, don't you? You've followed them, no doubt – with those all-seeing eyes of yours. I am the author of *The Prince of Darkness, A Study of Lord Byron as a Sexual Outcast, Baudelaire and the Satanists, Swinburne and the Divine Marquis de Sade.* Did your omniscience happen to notice my piece on 'Poetry of the Damned' last week in *The Times Lit. Supp.*? Did that raise a few celestial eyebrows, did it? [*Pause.*] You've very quiet. You think – I'm being frivolous, don't you? Luby flippant again. Luby doesn't take things seriously. Well, I *don't*! I have no intention of taking this seriously. This is an optical illusion. There's some quite simple scientific explanation. I tell you what it is. Exactly! It's a bad dream, brought on by over-indulgence in British Council sherry and too much of that dubious fish paste spread on cheesy biscuits. I am going to shut my eyes now and count to ten. [*He sits down on the bed and shuts his eyes.*] By the time I open them again you will have all gone away! Vanished! You ... You old Myth, you ... Fairy tales! *Opiate of the People!* One – two – three ...

FLETCHER [*sleepily; speaking with a Humberside accent, without opening his eyes*]: Who's that? Who?

LUBY: Four – five – six ...

FLETCHER: Gwen? Is that my little Gwenny ...?

LUBY: Seven – eight ...

FLETCHER: Alison ...? Jimbo. Is that you, Jim boy?

LUBY: Nine ... I said nine ...

FLETCHER: Just slipped into the chemist – on the hunt for Fly Death ...

LUBY: All right. Are you ready? Ten!

FLETCHER: Bloody Iti chemist. Pulled a knife on yours truly. I must've upset them somehow ...

LUBY: *Ten!* I said ten!

FLETCHER: Did you say ten?

LUBY: Vanish! Pack up your ridiculous harps and vanish!

FLETCHER [*opening his eyes and looking out at Luby*]: Look, friend. I'm not interfering with you, am I? Just had a spot of bother with one of the natives round in the chemist's.

[LUBY *also opens his eyes, and looks up at the ceiling.*]

LUBY: I don't believe it for a moment. You're still there! [*He stands to examine the ceiling more closely.*]

FLETCHER: Yes. And here I'll stay. Got me in the gut, most probably. All the same – I thought it'd've been more painful. I didn't feel much really. No pain to speak of ...

LUBY: Harps! I just can't bear the thought of the Archbishop of Canterbury arriving here. That awful smug 'I told you so' expression.

FLETCHER: Can you help me, friend?

[LUBY *looks at* FLETCHER, *then moves to him.*]

LUBY: It's a fellow soul. Calling me 'friend' ...

FLETCHER: Can you just help me get my bearings?

LUBY: 'Friend'? Is that what they call each other here? Like a Baptist congress in Philadelphia. [*Very depressed, he sits down on his bed.*]

FLETCHER: Pardon me, old man. Where are we?

LUBY: Oh, where do you think?

FLETCHER: Search me ...

LUBY: Look. Up there – look upwards. [*Pause.*] Well?

[FLETCHER *looks up at the ceiling. Pause. He is amazed.*]

FLETCHER: Oh. My God!

LUBY: Yours perhaps. He's never been mine.

FLETCHER [*in an awestruck whisper*]: Tell me frankly. Have we passed over?

LUBY: That would seem an appropriate cliché for an extremely trite situation.

[*Pause.* FLETCHER *climbs out of bed; he looks up at the ceiling.*]

FLETCHER [*awestruck*]: It's beautiful!

LUBY: You think so?

FLETCHER: Beautifully kept. Like the Municipal Gardens without the begonias.

LUBY: That seems a suitably depressing description.

FLETCHER: Quite a fair area of grass, isn't there?

LUBY: If you like grass there is quite a lot of it. Yes.

FLETCHER: Take a bit of mowing, that area of lawn.

LUBY: I don't imagine there's much else to do here. I see it as a perpetual English Sunday . . .

FLETCHER: Those angels. They look pleasant enough.

LUBY [*contemptuously*]: Pleasant! I have always preferred the corrupt innocence of those misnamed Ladies of Pleasure – Dark Angels. I have often missed stations – following one on the Northern Line . . .

FLETCHER: I imagine time will pass – very pleasantly up here.

LUBY: Oh, yes! Picture the evenings? Gounod's 'Ave Maria' on the West lawn and readings from *The Little Flowers of St Francis*.

FLETCHER [*suddenly shouting*]: Hallelujah!

LUBY [*revolted*]: Oh, please!

FLETCHER [*whispering*]: Isn't that what you're meant to say?

LUBY: I have no idea. I arrived here rather suddenly.

FLETCHER [*sitting down on his bed*]: You only recently – passed over?

LUBY: One moment I was taking sherry and cheesy biscuits with a perfectly civilized old trout from the American Library. We were discussing, as I remember it, the various sexual contretemps of the great Lord Byron and the theme of damnation in Romantic Poetry. Suddenly there was a cry of warning from a startled cleric who had disapproved of my lecture. 'Look out, chaps. The balcony's falling in!' I only had time for a last gulp of the South African Amontillado before they dumped me in this celestial kindergarten.

FLETCHER: You felt – no pain at all?

LUBY: Very little.

FLETCHER: It doesn't seem to hurt much. Not death.

LUBY: Oh, I agree. It's the life after that's such agony.

FLETCHER: You shouldn't say that!

LUBY: Why?

FLETCHER: It's ungrateful!

LUBY: I never asked to come here!

FLETCHER: Of course you didn't. It's an honour. Like sitting at the Master Mason's table at the annual dinner dance.

LUBY: That seems to sum it up pretty accurately.

FLETCHER: Be thankful. Look around you! It's just like the pictures in Sunday School.

LUBY: I know nothing about that, of course.

FLETCHER: Don't you remember them?

LUBY: My dear mother was Chairlady of the Dulwich Humanitarians. I'd've gone to Sunday School over her dead body.

FLETCHER: And now you've come here over yours! Pardon my sense of humour.

LUBY: No doubt your little jokes will make eternity pass extremely slowly.

FLETCHER: Eternity? I imagine we'll be here for quite some time.

LUBY: Not me. Not once they realize the mistake they're making.

FLETCHER: Well. We might as well get to know each other. The name's Fletcher. The boys call me Tommy. What's yours?

[Pause.]

LUBY: What? Oh, I'm Luby. Lewis Luby. Does it ring a bell?

FLETCHER: I'm afraid – not a tinkle.

LUBY: *The* Lewis Luby. Of *The Prince of Darkness, Lord Byron as a Sexual Outcast*.

FLETCHER: Unusual name.

LUBY: I'm an unusual person.

FLETCHER: I'm not. Very ordinary. Can't imagine why I should get sent here.

LUBY: Perhaps as a reward for an uneventful life.

FLETCHER: I haven't been *that* charitable. Odd flag on Life Boat Day, of course. Charity begins at home – and you need it after what the tax man leaves you. I had a diabolical coding!

LUBY: Mr Fletcher. I don't intend to spend the next ten thousand years discussing your income tax!

FLETCHER: Oh, I beat the P.A.Y.E. all right. Once I emigrated to the land of spaghetti and kissed the Inland Revenue goodbye. It seems they don't hold that against you. Not up here.

LUBY: Perhaps they don't know. The place doesn't look exactly staffed with Chartered Accountants.

FLETCHER: They know everything. And they forgive you. That's what it is. 'Course I've done a bit for export. That might count in my favour.

LUBY [*uninterestedly*]: Really?

FLETCHER: Meat pies and pin tables. I run the English café down by the old Marina. We do an all-in meal and a bingo evening plus amusements for ten thousand lire. We made a good thing of it.

LUBY: You think that earned you Salvation – like the Queen's reward for industry?

FLETCHER: What else worked it? I'm no saint.

LUBY: And I, Fletcher, am certainly a sinner.

FLETCHER: Ssh ...

LUBY: I have no intention of keeping quiet about it.

FLETCHER: No point in reminding Him, if it's all water under the bridge. No point in raising old embarrassments. That *is* God the Father, isn't it, Mr Luby? I mean from where we are now you don't see much past the sandal.

LUBY: I imagine He will be looking presently, in this direction.

FLETCHER: I thought I recognized Him, from the pictures ...

LUBY [*standing up and shouting at God's foot*]:

> '*Mais le Damné répond*
> *Toujours "Je ne veux pas!"*'

FLETCHER [*puzzled*]: What?

LUBY: 'The damned still answer
  We want no part of Heaven!'
  You have no French?

FLETCHER: None whatsoever.

LUBY: What is this place? A public park stocked with people who don't know their Baudelaire.

FLETCHER: Am I?

LUBY: What?

FLETCHER: Whatever you said.

LUBY: Oh, my God!

FLETCHER [*reverently*]: Well, at least you can pray. That's something.

LUBY: You'll be telling me next you are entirely ignorant of Lord B.

FLETCHER: Who?

LUBY: George Gordon Noel. The Lord Byron.

FLETCHER: The Lord Byron I know well.

LUBY: Oh, really? Are you one of his intimates, Fletcher? One of his devil-may-care cronies? Did you share the housemaids with his Lordship at Newstead Abbey, or the boys in Venice, or did you just drink and gamble the night away in his rooms in St James?

FLETCHER: It's a motel . . .

LUBY: What?

FLETCHER: The Lord Byron. The new motel, outside Nottingham, on the A46.

LUBY [*desperately*]: There is no culture here!

FLETCHER: A cosy sort of place. Me and my little Gwenny stayed there, on occasion. Double bed with shower and no luggage asked for.

LUBY: Lord Byron, Fletcher, has absolutely nothing to do with you and your little Gwenny. Lord Byron was a great poet who shouted his defiance at the heavens – and sinned gloriously. And I have lit candles at the altar of his wickedness in a hundred lectures specially given for the British Council – both sides of the Iron Curtain.

FLETCHER [*suspiciously*]: You give lectures?

LUBY: I prefer to think of them as small acts of liberation.

FLETCHER: With slides, would that be?

[*During the following speech* FLETCHER *looks more and more shocked.*]

LUBY [*pacing and gesturing eloquently*]: I do not need slides! I rely on words and the poet's great example. 'Experience', I tell my listeners, 'is the only duty of the artist. All experience is an arch where-through – glimmers the unknown truth. It is the duty of the artist to live life to the full!' I tell them quite honestly. His destiny and his curse! The poet must be mad, bad and dangerous to know. He finds his inspiration waking between two greasy whores in Seven Dials or watching the sun set over Mont Blanc – among the monks of Athos and the boy catamites of Syracuse, dancing in a Venetian carnival or vomiting in the gutters of Piccadilly.

FLETCHER [*appalled*]: You actually used that word?

LUBY: What word?

FLETCHER: 'Vomiting'.

LUBY: The divine nausea that follows each inspired Bacchanalia.

FLETCHER: Filthy!

LUBY: 'We gaze into a puddle – and see the reflections of the stars.'

FLETCHER: Mixed lectures, I imagine they are.

LUBY: As mixed as possible.

FLETCHER: You devil!

LUBY [*pleased*]: Thank you, Fletcher, I do my best. The devil has all the best lines in Milton . . .

FLETCHER: It's immoral!

LUBY: Art has no moral boundaries! That's what I tell them.

FLETCHER: Flaunting it. In public. Who pays for it? That's what I'd like to know.

LUBY: What?

FLETCHER: Who finances you – spreading that muck around the world? I know – Jo Muggins!

LUBY: Who?

FLETCHER: Me! The British Tax Payer!

LUBY: I thought you had resigned from that position . . .

FLETCHER: I'm still entitled to my voice, aren't I? As one of the silent majority.

LUBY: I think there may be some logical flaw in that statement.

FLETCHER: To see that certain standards are maintained! Suppose – suppose a child happened to walk into one of your lectures.

LUBY: Children seldom stray into talks on Romantic Poetry in a foreign language.

FLETCHER: A young girl might go in thinking it was Brownies ...

LUBY: Your ingenuity amazes me.

FLETCHER: Our kids are entitled to a little childhood, Mr Luby.

LUBY: I knew it! I knew heaven'd be like this! Let's hope Mrs Whitehouse isn't feeling seedy.

[LUBY *lies on the bed as if suddenly bored with the argument.*]

FLETCHER: Whatever I've done. I haven't gone around trumpeting it from the podium. I haven't flashed it on the screen in the form of lantern slides.

LUBY: I told you. There are *no* lantern slides!

FLETCHER: I'm not setting up as perfect but at least I've caused no offence ...

LUBY: I imagine your life has been as free from offence as the expurgated edition of *Little Women*.

FLETCHER: I mean, I may have taken Gwenny down to the motel a weekend or two. But we did our best not to cause embarrassment. I always treated Gwen like a sister.

LUBY: Hardly a romantic approach to your mistress.

FLETCHER: I don't see why. After all she *was* my sister.

[*Pause.* LUBY *sits up slowly and looks at* FLETCHER.]

LUBY: She was – *what?*

FLETCHER: My sister.

LUBY: Mr Fletcher. Why are you telling me this?

FLETCHER: I don't want you to get the idea I'm not completely normal.

LUBY [*puzzled*]: Normal?

FLETCHER [*determinedly, standing up*]: I mean, a man with just the usual desires and instincts. I can't stand filth, that's all. There's not a lecture you can take the family to these days. It's shocking!

LUBY: It was your sister you took away ...?

FLETCHER [*looking up at the ceiling*]: It's been forgiven, surely? Seeing I'm here.

LUBY: Your sister Gwen?

FLETCHER: Ten years younger than me – and slim as a daffodil. The flesh is weak, Mr Luby.

LUBY: I imagine so. Given the opportunity.

FLETCHER: Our Gwen was always a nervous child in company. She'd sit at a family tea as good as gold, never get a word out of her except 'thank you' for a piece of cake. But when it was over she'd be out with me for a walk along the sands dancing like a wild thing and laughing at the aunts.

LUBY [*confused*]: You lived by the sea?

FLETCHER: Humberside. You know it at all?

LUBY: Hardly at all.

FLETCHER: Fine sands. Little dunes with tufts of grass on them. Naturally one thing led to another.

LUBY: I've found – one thing has so often led to nothing.

FLETCHER: I could make Gwen laugh so easily. You know how it is. That's all you want, isn't it, a bit of a laugh and then you're away. Any woman's the same.

LUBY: My own wife doesn't laugh very much. She comes from Austria. [*Pause.*] But, Mr Fletcher. Are you quite sure – you read no poetry?

FLETCHER: None whatsoever. I hardly get time for the newspaper.

LUBY: Then how do you explain it?

FLETCHER: Explain what, Mr Luby?

LUBY: That in certain respects you and the great Lord B ... Well, in *one* respect at least ... [*Hopefully*] I assume this remarkable close family relationship has been your only peccadillo?

FLETCHER [*sitting down on his bed, facing* LUBY]: I was never *really* unfaithful to Gwenny ...

LUBY: Ah ...

FLETCHER: Not in my heart, I wasn't.

LUBY: Your heart?

FLETCHER: I mean, after I married Alison ...

LUBY: Alison?

FLETCHER: The present Mrs Fletcher. She's a qualified book-keeper is Alison. Helped me build up the business ...

LUBY: A mathematician?

FLETCHER: Computer sharp.

LUBY: Hard, cold, angular? The Princess of the Parallelograms?

FLETCHER: Soft, dark and kindness itself.

LUBY: But in her heart somewhere – a chip of ice? Not a passionate woman, your mathematical wife?

FLETCHER: Nothing wrong with my Alison, in the bed department.

LUBY: Nothing?

FLETCHER: Warm, crisp and regular. Like a slice of breakfast toast.

LUBY: But your little Gwen . . .

FLETCHER: It was the laughs I had with Gwenny. She saw the joke in everything. Whatever I said I got the laughs out of her, like hitting the jackpot.

LUBY: So you still went walking across the sands?

FLETCHER: Most Fridays. When Alison had an evening casting up the books.

LUBY: Tell me, Mr Fletcher. Tell me quite honestly. Weren't you afraid of *La Grande Scandale*?

FLETCHER: People talking?

LUBY: Exactly!

FLETCHER: I took precautions . . .

LUBY: You were discreet?

FLETCHER: It was the year I heard a certain whispering at a Chamber of Commerce function. I had to put an end to the rumours. I arranged for Gwen to marry Jimbo.

LUBY [*frowning*]: I don't think we've heard of Jimbo, have we?

FLETCHER: Jim Penrose. We were at school together.

LUBY: A lifelong friend?

FLETCHER: He was a lad, was Jimbo. Good at everything!

LUBY: First prize for Algebra *and* on the cricket field?

FLETCHER: Hit like a County player. Cut into the water like a swallow, top of the wall bars as soon as look at you – and if it was any kind of mischief . . .

LUBY: Stink bombs, itching powder? Plastic doggy-do on the altar steps . . .?

FLETCHER: Lovers! Jim had all the lovers . . .

LUBY: You went to a co-educational school, then? Just like mine . . .

FLETCHER: One sex strictly. You never got a sight of a girl at the Grammar.

LUBY: So your Jim's lovers . . .

FLETCHER: Queued up! I was lucky to be one of them. I was a duffer at cricket . . .

LUBY: And Jim confined himself, mainly to the first eleven?

FLETCHER: I was the exception. I don't know why. My sense of humour must have tickled him . . .

LUBY [*disapprovingly, standing up*]: Your sense of humour seems to have brought you many opportunities . . .

FLETCHER: Oh yes – I think it's because of that Jim stuck to me, even after school . . .

LUBY: You continued to meet?

FLETCHER: At Masonic functions, old school reunions. Jim went into the motor trade. I was in catering. There was bags of opportunities . . .

LUBY: I'm sorry. I begin to be appalled.

FLETCHER: We took up angling. Jim made some fantastic catches, naturally I was a duffer. If anyone saw us walking up the sand together of an evening we were out after bait. You know, those small worms that make wedding cake decorations on the sand . . .

LUBY: I *don't* know.

FLETCHER: You put down a drop of salt and fool the worms into thinking the tide's come in . . .

LUBY: Cunning, no doubt! So you had the best of three worlds?

FLETCHER: It was like a fast ride on a motor bike with Gwen. And my Alison was always a comfort. But when it came to Jimbo . . .

LUBY: Well?

FLETCHER: Jim was – like keeping young forever.

LUBY [*turning on* FLETCHER, *horrified*]: So it was Jim you persuaded to marry Gwen?

FLETCHER: When people started talking. It didn't make any difference, of course, not to any of us!

LUBY: Life continued – much as before?

FLETCHER: Business as usual. Until the tax man got at us. Then I moved them all out here.

LUBY: Everyone?

FLETCHER: The whole family! We work as a team.

LUBY: Obviously.

FLETCHER: Down by the old Marina! *La Trattoria Tommy.* Gwenny's behind the bar and Jim's clickety click.

LUBY: So I understood you to say.

FLETCHER: He calls the numbers on Thursdays. And Alison does the books, naturally. They'll be wondering where I've got to . . .

LUBY [*sarcastically*]: I really can't imagine what they'll do without you.

FLETCHER: No. They'd all be glad, though. To know I arrived here safely . . .

LUBY: I should think they'll be astonished!

FLETCHER: Astonished? Why? I've done nothing to be ashamed of.

LUBY: Nothing to be . . .? Mr Fletcher, I told you. I'm not easily shocked! In fact I should have said up till now I was unshockable. But I find your conduct inexcusable!

FLETCHER: *They* didn't. Not up here.

LUBY: What they think or do up here really doesn't affect me in the slightest. What you have revealed is a life of pure self-indulgence!

FLETCHER [*standing up and facing him*]: What about that Lord B of yours you're always on about? Boys in Venice – greasy whores . . .

LUBY: The poet Byron lived for his art!

FLETCHER: Didn't stop his fun, though, did it?

LUBY: Fun? What do you mean, fun? It was his martyrdom. So far as I can see you have indulged your appalling sensuality simply because you enjoy it . . .

FLETCHER: Seems a good reason . . .

LUBY: And you have not produced from your sordid intrigues one sonnet! Not a quatrain. Not even taken time in your prancing from bed to bed, regardless of age and sex, to jot down a single rhyming couplet. How can you justify it?

FLETCHER: I kept them happy.

LUBY: Happiness – is not everything. Are artists happy?

FLETCHER: I was.

LUBY: Your conduct strikes me as entirely selfish.

FLETCHER: I was thinking of *them*.

LUBY: Oh, really?

FLETCHER: I'm not saying I've always kept on the straight and narrow. A man has to have *something* outside his family life.

LUBY: Even with your extended family?

FLETCHER: But when I thought that business with young Claudia got out of hand ...

LUBY: *Claudia*? [*He turns away from him, disgusted.*] Your life swells to epic proportions, Fletcher. With a cast of thousands!

FLETCHER: Her husband runs the chemist's down the Corso Garibaldi. We get all sorts of insects down the coast in the summer. I often call in for a bomb of Fly Death when I'm in town. Good stuff, that Fly Death. I can recommend it ...

LUBY: Mr Fletcher! [*Turning back to him*] Now you're here – now by some extraordinary latitude on the part of the authorities you've scraped your way into Heaven – I imagine you'll have as little use for Fly Death as for your undoubted talent for intrigue and romance ...!

FLETCHER: It was all right at first. We had a lot of fun. She'd lock the shop up and we'd go in there, behind the bead curtain. But then she started coming down the Trat on Sundays, making scenes. One day she upset the Bingo. I couldn't have Alison worried.

LUBY: Or Gwen? Or Jimbo, presumably?

FLETCHER: I called to tell her it was all over. She ran to get the knife out of the kitchen and came back screaming. Luckily I can't speak much of the lingo.

LUBY: You might have been shocked?

FLETCHER: It was uncalled for, what she did. Definitely uncalled for. I hardly felt it. That's what surprised me.

[FLETCHER *sits down on his bed again as if feeling weak.*]

LUBY: 'How foreign women revenge'. If you'd bothered to read Lord Byron ...

FLETCHER: They don't watch what they're doing. Seen them drive, haven't you? She wasn't in full control of the knife.

LUBY: There seems to be a certain natural justice ...

FLETCHER: Justice?

LUBY: You were heading for trouble, if you want my opinion. You'd simply got away with it too long.

FLETCHER: But I thought you took the view . . .

LUBY: A poet's life without a line of poetry to show for it! Oh yes, Mr Fletcher, I'm afraid you rather had it coming.

FLETCHER: I'm no worse than the rest of you.

LUBY [*with growing indignation*]: We don't all flee the country, Mr Fletcher, to avoid the tax man and set up unisex harems in foreign bingo halls. Incest and homosexuality are not our regular diversions, like the *Times* crossword. We don't drop into the chemist's in the afternoon for a small packet of aspirins and a spot of adultery.

FLETCHER: You must have done it often.

LUBY [*outraged*]: I *must*! Must I? Let me tell you, Fletcher. With the single exception of Mrs Luby I've never had a woman in my life! [*He sits down on his bed.*]

[*Pause. Then* FLETCHER *bursts into loud, uncontrollable laughter.*]

Have I said something particularly amusing?

FLETCHER [*trying to control himself*]: You – old sinner, you! 'The devil has all the best lines'. Isn't that what you told me . . .?

LUBY: I was discussing the poetry of Milton . . .

FLETCHER [*incredulously*]: You mean *no one* – only your good lady?

LUBY: No one else at all. [*Pause.*] Naturally, I'm sensitive about it. [*Pause.*] It's not the sort of thing, one likes to have generally known.

FLETCHER: They'd think you were kinky down our Rotary! [*Starting to laugh again*] I'm sorry.

LUBY: I shouldn't have told you. You led me into it.

FLETCHER: But it's unbelievable!

LUBY: Yes, it is rather. I suppose it is.

FLETCHER: I'm beginning to think – you haven't ever lived, Mr Luby!

LUBY: I was meaning to. I was looking forward to it . . .

FLETCHER: But you must have had bags of opportunity, from your early years.

LUBY: Not really a great deal of opportunity.

FLETCHER: I mean, I was brought up strictly Chapel. My Dad never missed the Radio Parson. But *you*, Mr Luby. With a mother who let you off Sunday School. An unbeliever!

LUBY: Mother! Poor Mother. She put no moral pressure on me. She gave me no rules. She only said that if I did anything 'ugly', it would make her very sad.

FLETCHER: And did you?

LUBY: Oh, believe me, Mr Fletcher. I spent my early years desperately hunting for an opportunity to make Mother sad.

FLETCHER: So as soon as you got to your school ...

LUBY: She sent me to a co-educational day place. Run by Quakers.

FLETCHER: You mean, girls in the classes?

LUBY: I was a nervous boy, desperately shy and frightened of cricket balls. The girls were only interested in sport ...

FLETCHER: Like my Jimbo.

LUBY: They bowled me out first ball in the nets and from then on ignored me.

FLETCHER: So – you never took advantage?

LUBY: Nothing happened. Mother remained imperturbably happy.

FLETCHER: But some time, surely ...

LUBY: I hesitated. It seemed for an eternity.

FLETCHER: Don't want to waste your time. Life's too short.

LUBY: Oh, I agree. At last I decided that I was the Captain of my Soul. I'd take my life and throw it on the table. To win or lose all! I would enlist in the Army of the Condemned! I remember it as if it were yesterday. I put on a clean white shirt, open at the neck with a paisley scarf – part of Mother's personal effects. I splashed on eau-de-cologne – it was before the age of after-shave, you follow me!

FLETCHER: Pleased to. I've made similar preparations.

LUBY: It was a poetry evening at the Literary Institute. Mulled wine was being served, and Dundee cake.

FLETCHER: Some kind of an orgy? You'll get that with poets ...

LUBY: I looked round. It was the period of dirndl skirts and embroidered blouses. The lady poets looked big and healthy, glowing, I thought, like Byron's peasant maids ... 'With breasts never made to suckle slaves . . .' Mother was forgotten! I owed experience a debt which could only be paid with my virginity.

FLETCHER: And you were how old, exactly?

LUBY: Exactly? It was my thirty-first birthday. I looked about the room and prepared to make a decision. The decision that would alter my whole life! The green dirndl in the corner, I thought – or the soft brown eyes, the red sweater and strong white teeth about to sink into a doorstep of cake . . . I paused to make my selection. And then . . .

FLETCHER: Then?

LUBY: A hand fell on my arm like an arrest. I was offered a glass of mulled wine in an Austrian accent. I had been selected.

FLETCHER: By?

LUBY: Sophie. The present Mrs Luby. She simply wouldn't take 'no' for an answer.

FLETCHER: And you?

LUBY: Married her. It was what she preferred.

FLETCHER: Well, I'm sure you found some sort of occasion. Some sort of evening off. The Masons perhaps, or the Rotary. Then slip away early . . .

LUBY: I never once deceived her.

FLETCHER: Never on any occasion?

LUBY: Never.

FLETCHER: Let's get this clear . . .

LUBY: Yes . . .

FLETCHER: You were totally inexperienced at the age of thirty-one?

LUBY: Totally.

FLETCHER: And then – it was only your wife . . .?

LUBY: No one but Sophie. You've forced the disgraceful truth out of me.

[FLETCHER *stands up and looks up at the ceiling thoughtfully*.]

FLETCHER: No wonder they put you in here, Mr Luby.

LUBY [*standing up, outraged*]: Don't say it! I am here because of my appalling record. I am one of the sexually underprivileged. It was my upbringing – the accident of myopia and

a slight stoop. Even so I could have risen above my disadvan-
tages. I could never have been Byron, of course – but a more
modest form of dissolute poet – Ernest Dawson, perhaps. I
could have managed. 'I have been faithful to thee, Cynara, in
my fashion ...' Sophie wouldn't put up with infidelity.

FLETCHER: How did she stop you?

LUBY [*sitting down; disconsolately*]: She said that it would make
her sad.

FLETCHER: Like your ...

LUBY: Her sadness was terrible! Days of thunder and the rivulets
of tears. Our living-room became a sort of wailing wall on the
one occasion I was late home.

FLETCHER: You'd been following those Ladies of Pleasure ...

LUBY: For a station or two on the tube only. I came to my senses
around Mornington Crescent.

FLETCHER: But still she carried on.

LUBY: I never kept her waiting after that ...

FLETCHER: But when you came away. Like on lectures?

[FLETCHER *sits down beside* LUBY *on* LUBY's *bed*.]

LUBY: She expected a postcard daily. I never had the courage to
deceive her on a postcard. You see what my life's been, Mr
Fletcher?

FLETCHER: I suppose you could say, on the quietish side.

LUBY: To be landed here. In this uneventful eternity!

FLETCHER: Like finding the bar closed before you ever got round
to ordering a drink.

LUBY: Mr Fletcher ...

FLETCHER: Yes?

LUBY: You know, that really puts it rather well.

FLETCHER: Thank you.

[*Pause*.]

LUBY: I was no doubt a little hard on you.

FLETCHER: Think nothing of it.

LUBY: A little – over-critical.

FLETCHER: That surprised me, rather.

LUBY: You must understand – I'm a little edgy. A little piqued.
I have suffered – a considerable disappointment.

FLETCHER: Disappointment, Mr Luby?

LUBY: Finding myself – so unexpectedly in heaven ...

FLETCHER: Indeed, yes. I do see. I see it must be, something of a let-down for you.

LUBY: To be unexpectedly taken off – in a state of innocence! To pass from one uneventful eternity to another ... To be called to rest, Mr Fletcher, before one has a chance of getting tired.

[*Pause.*]

FLETCHER [*yawning and stretching*]: I think I was about ready for it. [*He moves over to his bed.*]

LUBY: What?

FLETCHER [*getting back into his bed, pulling up the covers over him, preparing for sleep*]: The whistle. I've enjoyed the game, of course. Every minute of it. Alison and Claudia and Jimbo and Gwendoline. Especially young Gwen. But they seem to want more out of you as the years go by. It even got just that much more of an effort to make young Gwen laugh. Yes. I'm not sorry to be packing it all in.

LUBY: 'We'll go no more a roving ...'

FLETCHER: I'd like a chance of sleeping alone. After all these years.

LUBY: You should get plenty of that up here.

FLETCHER: To stretch out your legs right across the bed, to suck boiled sweets and read the Sunday papers. Not to have to climb the stairs each night to a kind of athletic meeting at Wembley Stadium.

LUBY: Were they so demanding?

FLETCHER: Time consuming, I'd say. I got no gardening done.

LUBY: 'Though the night was made for loving
　　　And the moon shines bright ...'

FLETCHER: I'd like to have got in more gardening.

LUBY: Perhaps they'll let you help out with the lawns.

FLETCHER: I'd appreciate that.

LUBY: 'Though the sword outwears its sheath
　　　And the soul wears out the breast.'

FLETCHER [*suspiciously*]: What's that mean?

LUBY: What?

FLETCHER: 'The sword outwears the sheath.' What's that intended for?

LUBY: I imagine it's symbolic. Of the poet's virility . . .

FLETCHER [*with deep disapproval*]: I thought so!

LUBY: 'And the heart must pause to breathe
      And love itself have rest.'

FLETCHER: Disgusting! That's what it is. 'The sword wears out the sheath.' Ought to be put a stop to! [*He closes his eyes.*]

LUBY: 'Though the night was made for loving
      And the day returns too soon.'

FLETCHER [*his voice sounding faint*]: Filth!

LUBY: 'Yes, we'll go no more a roving.' [*Shouting*] Oh God! Don't you understand? *I never went!* [*More quietly pleading*] Let me out. Please. God. Let me back again.

[*The sound of Gounod's 'Ave Maria' is heard.*]

No! I won't believe it. I won't . . .

[LUBY *gets back into bed quickly, pulls the bedclothes over his head and lies down. The lights, including the light on the ceiling, fade almost to darkness.*]

[*As the light fades so the* NUN *moves in and we see her move the screen round* FLETCHER'*s bed so that he is hidden from the audience. Darkness. 'Ave Maria' grows louder. The light changes to pale daylight. The ceiling is shadowy and unlit. We can see the surrounding ward. The* YOUNG ITALIAN'*s transistor is on, playing 'Ave Maria'. The* NUN *is standing by the doorway. She claps her hands severely.*]

NUN: *Silencio! Il radio. Il dottore arriva!*

[*The* YOUNG ITALIAN *clicks off his radio.*
The DOCTOR *comes in briskly. The* NUN *goes. The* DOCTOR *moves to* LUBY'*s bed and touches his shoulder.*]

DOCTOR: Good morning, Mr Luby. Feeling a little better?

LUBY [*peering miserably out of the bed covers*]: I'll never feel better here. Never . . .

DOCTOR: All the same, you seem to be still with us. Lying on your back, that's good. Admiring the ceiling?

LUBY [*puzzled*]: The ceiling?

DOCTOR: I like it best in the early morning. Before the guides come – and the tours. When you are alone watching it one almost feels, does one not, transported to Paradise.

LUBY: *Almost?*

DOCTOR: Such is the power of a great work of art.

LUBY: Work of art. Is that all it is?

DOCTOR: *All?* Did you say all? And you a distinguished lecturer. For the British Council. What should we prize more highly – than a superb mural, a masterpiece of the *cinquecento*, the *chef d'oeuvre* of a son of this very city, Bernadino di Taddeo. Nicknamed the lame one.

LUBY: It's *not* heaven?

DOCTOR: Nicknamed 'Il Zoppo'.

LUBY [*sitting up*]: Where am I then? *Where?* If it's not heaven it must be ... Tell me – tell me, my dear fellow. Do you happen to know a Lord Byron? He must be here somewhere. A pale gentleman with black curls. You haven't seen him? Possibly tricked out in Greek National Dress ...

DOCTOR: Please, Mr Luby ...

LUBY: Not with a limp exactly. But with, shall we say, a slight impediment of the leg?

DOCTOR: Calm yourself! I shall have to ask the Nursing Sister to give you a suppository.

LUBY [*convinced*]: Then I *am* in Hell ...

DOCTOR: Don't talk nonsense. You are nowhere of the sort.

LUBY: Nowhere ...

DOCTOR: You are in the Hospital for Transients and the Urban Poor. Where they brought you last night. After the balcony collapsed ...

LUBY: What exactly are you trying to tell me?

DOCTOR: Courage, Mr Luby. You're making a good recovery.

LUBY: Are you dropping the hint – I'm alive?

DOCTOR: As alive, Mr Luby, as ever.

LUBY: Alive! [*Excitedly*] Oh, no. More than ever ...! More! I shall be more alive than ever now. Much more! I have wasted my time! Totally wasted. There's a little more time, isn't there? What do they call it in bars? Drinking up time! No, naturally. You wouldn't know that expression. And I tell you,

Doctor. I promise you. I shall drink up everything. Every little drop available!

[*The* NUN *returns and stands by the* DOCTOR.]

For – instance. Let me think now. What they might be serving. No sister. I have no sister. Mother has a lot to answer for! Never mind! The world is full. I shall ask everyone! What do ten refusals matter, ten slaps in the face? Many will refuse but many will accept. Many will be delighted to accept. What is there here? What's ready to hand? Nuns. Well, perhaps not nuns. Not nuns to start with. But there are – chemist shops no doubt. Doctor – no doubt you know the Corso Garibaldi. I must go down to the chemist's.

[LUBY *starts to try to get out of bed. The* DOCTOR *forces him back as the* NUN *whispers a message to the* DOCTOR.]

DOCTOR: Mr Luby! What are you trying to do?

[*The* DOCTOR *nods to the* NUN, *who goes back to the doorway.* LUBY *is still struggling to get out of bed.*]

LUBY: To enjoy a number of experiences, Doctor! Before it's altogether too late. To collect a few memories, to warm my old age. Am I still to go to bed with nothing but my wife and Enid Starkie's *Life of Baudelaire*? Let me get up, Doctor. I can walk. I suppose I can walk ... Is there somewhere here to get a bath – a clean shirt and a whiff of eau-de-cologne? *Let me get up!*

DOCTOR: Please! Don't disturb yourself, Mr Luby.

[*The* NUN *comes back with* SOPHIE LUBY, *a formidable-looking lady wearing a lot of scarves and beads.*]

DOCTOR: Look – Sister is bringing you a visitor. A lady.

LUBY: To visit me? A lady? What lady?

SOPHIE [*in a rather hearty, cheerful but commanding Austrian accent*]: Lie down now, Lewis. There's a good chap!

LUBY [*quietly*]: Sophie! You shouldn't have come.

SOPHIE: That's better. Lewis, how could you make me so terribly sad?

[SOPHIE *sits down beside the bed. The* DOCTOR *smiles at* SOPHIE, *and leaves with the* NUN.]

All night in the aeroplane. In the bus also. I was crying. Crying ... [*Starting to get tearful*] Oh, Lewis. Why should you do such a thing to your Sophie?

LUBY: Please don't do that! Try not to weep! I didn't hurl myself from the balcony, you know. It wasn't an act of deliberate defenestration. Designed to cause you distress! In fact, I might say, the whole thing came as a total surprise to me.

SOPHIE [*determinedly*]: You must not go on these tours again.

LUBY [*surprised*]: I mustn't?

SOPHIE: These lectures! For you they are far too dangerous. I have decided with the lady from the British Council. They will keep you at home now. I have had you grounded, old chap.

LUBY: Home? No, Sophie. Please. I can't stay at home. You see, after this – after this life – it seems we can expect ... nothing very exciting. I've only got a few years. To make the best of it.

SOPHIE: But it will be exciting, Lewis. I have thought it all out. You shall stay at home and write the definitive book on your old chum, the great Lord Byron. Your beloved chap! I will help you. I will type out all your references on little cards. I will keep it systematic! We will have everything in alphabetical order – like for instance his debts – his incest – his homosexual tendencies ... Oh, Lewis. I will be your right-hand man!

LUBY: But Sophie. I would only experience sin in a card index.

SOPHIE: Well, of course. We would work together. I would have you at home at lunchtime. I could get us a salad.

LUBY [*bitterly*]: A salad! And in the evenings what would we look forward to?

SOPHIE: I make a little chicken dish maybe, how you like it. We'll get some new records for the winter – and books. There are still so many books for us to read together, Lewis. I have been thinking. Should we explore together the relationship of Rimbaud and Verlaine? A couple of queer fish, these two. After your own heart, eh?

LUBY [*depressed*]: We shall sit together, reading books in the evenings.

SOPHIE: Yes, Lewis. You won't go away from me again! Not ever. Won't that be heaven?

[*Pause, then* LUBY *answers her, desperate.*]

LUBY: Heaven?

SOPHIE [*laughing*]: Afraid! Don't be afraid, Lewis. We'll have such a perfect time ...

LUBY: Perfect! For all eternity. I think – I need a little advice. Mr Fletcher ...

SOPHIE: Who? Who do you want?

LUBY: There was a man here with me. In the next bed. Mr Fletcher. [*He looks at the screen round* FLETCHER's *bed.*]

SOPHIE: Who?

LUBY [*getting out of bed*]: An Englishman. An extraordinary man really ...

SOPHIE [*standing up, protesting*]: Lewis! You're not well ... You ...

[*Ignoring her,* LUBY *crosses to the screen.*]

LUBY: Gave his name as Fletcher. [*He pulls the screen aside. The bed is stripped and empty. The blankets neatly folded. He calls out.*] Sister! *Sorella! Senta!* Nurse!

[*The* NUN *enters and goes to him.*]

NUN: *Eccomi, signore.*

LUBY: *Sorella! Dove l'Inghlese ... Dove il signore ...* Tommy Fletcher?

NUN: *Il signore Fletcher e morte.*

LUBY: What? Come?

NUN: *Sta notte. E morte. Scusa, signore.*

LUBY: What?

SOPHIE: Dead, Lewis. She told you he was dead.

[*He sits down hopelessly, looking at the empty bed.*]

LUBY: Fletcher dead! And I'm alive. Harmlessly alive. You know what I have discovered? Everything *interesting* happens to Fletcher!

[*As* LUBY *looks at* FLETCHER's *bed the lights fade on every area of the stage except for the empty bed, which remains lit until a quick black-out, and —*

the curtain falls.]

THE PRINCE OF DARKNESS

The Prince of Darkness was first produced at the Greenwich Theatre on 28 May 1976 with the following cast:

THE REVEREND GAVIN FABER	*Peter Woodthorpe*
THE REVEREND A. K. BULSTRODE	*Denholm Elliott*
MADGE FABER	*Eleanor Bron*
THE BISHOP	*Trevor Baxter*
MR SLOCUM, a fishmonger	*Alan Dudley*

The play directed by John Tydeman
Setting by Peter Rice

Scene: The play takes place in the Rectory of St Barnabas Without, in South London.

Time: The present.

SCENE ONE

The ground floor of a large and down-at-heel Rectory in South London. Centre stage, the front door and part of the hall. The foot of a staircase near the front door. Left of it we can see part of a dingy kitchen – a bit of a table and a sink, all stacked with dirty plates as if the washing up hasn't been done for a long time. We can also see a massive old fridge with its back to us. Right of the hall we see almost all the main living and dining room. Various contemporary trends have washed over this room – and now the Habitat furniture is somewhat collapsed. There is a hi-fi, a dining table and chairs, a sofa, big cushions on the floor, a gas fire and a huge notice board with psychedelic posters announcing various discos and trendy parish events. A big window.

The play starts in darkness and loud noise – the build up to the opening crescendo of A Night at the Opera *by Queen. In the kitchen a despondent-looking middle-aged woman in nondescript clothes, who once was beautiful, is dabbing a dish mop ineffectively at a tea cup. She is* MADGE FABER, *the Rector's wife. The music is played at enormous volume. As* FREDDIE MERCURY *starts to sing 'Death on Two Legs' the stage lightens gradually and we see in front of the large hi-fi a figure in black trousers and a black high-necked sweater jerking convulsively to the music, his back towards us. 'Death on Two Legs' reaches the crescendo of the first verse.*

FREDDIE MERCURY [*singing on record*]:
>'Death on two legs
>You're tearing me apart!
>Death on two legs
>You never had a heart of your own . . .'

[*During the singing, almost drowned by it, there's a sound of a front door bell.* MADGE *comes out of the kitchen and opens the front door. A man comes in. He is wearing old grey flannel trousers and a tweed coat with leather patches and a dog collar. He is the* REVEREND A. K. BULSTRODE. *He is carrying a large kit bag and he salutes* MADGE *in the hall.*]

BULSTRODE: A. K. Bulstrode. Reporting for duty. [*He shuts the door.*] Remarkably hot this evening.

MADGE [*points to the living room*]: You're to go in there. [*She takes the kit bag from him.*] I'll put this up in your room.

BULSTRODE: No, I say, ma'am. Allow me . . .

MADGE [*dragging the kit bag towards the staircase*]: It's all right.

BULSTRODE: It's no weather for humping gear. Let me help at least . . .

MADGE: Why should you help me? Nobody does. [*She points listlessly to the living-room door.*] In there!

[*She goes off up the hall stairs dragging the kit bag.* BULSTRODE *approaches the door, listens for a moment to the mounting yells of* MERCURY. *His knock is drowned in the noise.*]

FREDDIE MERCURY [*on record*]:
>   'You're just an old barrow boy
>   Have you found a new toy.
>   To replace me . . .'

[BULSTRODE *pushes open the door and goes into the living room.*]

FREDDIE MERCURY [*singing*]:
>   'But now you can kiss my ass goodbye!'

BULSTRODE: What's that infernal racket?

[*The dancing figure stops and turns to face* BULSTRODE *in surprise. We now see that his black roll-neck sweater is cut away at the front to reveal a discreet dog collar. He is the* REVEREND GAVIN FABER, *Rector of the parish.*]

BULSTRODE: Club night for the local delinquents?

[GAVIN *goes to the hi-fi and switches it off.*]

GAVIN: Actually it was the Queen.

BULSTRODE: Well, it didn't sound in the least bit like her. Well now, sir, when do we get operational?

GAVIN: Excuse me?

BULSTRODE: This is just the sort of parish that offers a real challenge . . . to a curate of riper years. Down at the depot the other rookies envied me ... 'Your C.O. is a great rector,' they told me. Gavin Faber of St Bernard's ...

GAVIN: Saint Barnabas. Saint Barnabas Without ... [*He gives a small nervous giggle.*] Without what? That's what I always want to know.

BULSTRODE [*very serious*]: Without the walls, isn't it, sir? Without the city boundaries?

GAVIN [*vague*]: Yes, I suppose that's all it is ...

BULSTRODE: Out in the woglands ... I suppose you might say.

GAVIN [*shocked*]: No. I certainly shouldn't say that, not ever.

BULSTRODE: Plenty of scope for missionary work round here, I imagine. I am sure I heard tom-toms beating through Camberwell ...

GAVIN [*moving away from him*]: Oh dear, oh dear. One must be tolerant – even of intolerance. Remarkably close this evening. The weather ...

BULSTRODE: And I suppose they get up to it like rabbits ... whenever the barometer rises.

GAVIN [*severely*]: There's a lot that happens in this parish, I am sure you'll learn, that one has to be very, very tolerant about.

[MADGE *comes down the stairs into the kitchen and starts to tidy up ineffectively.*]

BULSTRODE: You mean sin, Wing-Co.?

GAVIN: Well now, sin. That's not a word we find very *useful* in the Church nowadays.

BULSTRODE: I am not trained to be tolerant of sin, Rector. It's just not part of my training. You know what we did with sin in F for Freddie Squadron? We used to go out every night after sin – and whack it on the head with about five tons of high explosive. [*He takes out a pipe and starts to fill it.*] You don't mind, do you?

GAVIN [*nervous smile*]: Mind what? Your pipe or your theology?

BULSTRODE: The old Three Nuns. I never got much of a smoke out of theology.

GAVIN: Look here, Anthony.

BULSTRODE [*firmly*]: A.K.

GAVIN: Andrew ...?

BULSTRODE: Let's stick to A.K., shall we? I don't suppose you want to get too familiar with the Junior Ranks ... A. K. Bulstrode. And to me you'll always be 'Sir', with all due respect, Rector.

GAVIN: Sir – if you insist ... [*Feeling uneasily round his dog collar*] Oppressive! There must be thunder in the air ...

> [*In the kitchen* MADGE *groans and sits at the table, her head in her hands.*]

GAVIN: I'm sure that now you've been sent to us ...

BULSTRODE: *Seconded.*

GAVIN: ... as curate, we'll find lots of useful work for you to do. Of a non-controversial nature.

BULSTRODE: Oh, I'm not afraid of work, sir. Which is why I welcome a tough posting! You should have seen the shambles they'd got into at R.A.F. Dungeness. As I said to the Wing-Co., we're going to stamp out the Prince of Darkness here, sir. Even if it means closing the Naafi ...

> [*The phone rings.* GAVIN *picks it up.*]

GAVIN: Excuse me. [*To the phone*] Gavin Faber here. St Barnabas Without. Oh, hello Peter. The 'Bish' wants to speak to me ...?

> [BULSTRODE *has moved very close to him and listens in awe.*]

BULSTRODE: The Supremo ...!

GAVIN: Martin ...?

BULSTRODE: Sorry. None of my business. Make myself scarce. [*He moves away and starts to look at the notices on the notice board.*]

> [*In the kitchen* MADGE *gets up, starts to make a pile of dirty plates in the sink.*]

GAVIN: *How* are you, Martin? Yes ... yes. No, not busy at all. Just settling in a new curate ... Riper years ... Sympatico? Well, he seems to have a vivid memory of World War II. Of course I think the 'Interdenominational Gay Front' is a super idea, Martin. Count me in committee-wise. Absolutely! What, you'll be passing us by on your way to Telly Centre? They don't *feed* you before the 'Epilogue'? Well, of course, I am sure Madge'd be delighted. It'll just be pot luck ...

[*In the kitchen* MADGE *opens a rusty pedal bin with her foot and drops the pile of plates into it with a resounding crash.* GAVIN *covers the mouthpiece for a moment with his hand.* BULSTRODE *doesn't react, he is examining the notice board.* MADGE *stands motionless looking down into the tidy bin, one hand clasped to her forehead.*]

GAVIN [*to phone*]: About eight o'clock then? Absolutely *super*, Martin. [*He puts down the phone.*]

BULSTRODE [*looking at the notice board*]: The good old notice board, I see, with all the briefings.

GAVIN [*puts down the phone, as if alarmed by his action*]: I've asked the Bishop to supper. [*Pause.*] Oh dear. I'll have to break it to Madge.

BULSTRODE [*reading the notices on the board*]: Tactile Communication ... Group Therapy. The Bondage Society.

GAVIN: Our Church functions!

BULSTRODE: Gay Get-together. At least that sounds cheerful.

GAVIN [*trying to reassure himself*]: Martin will take us as we come. He's such a *super* person. Not the least bit of *side* about being a Bishop.

[BULSTRODE *looks at a notice and reads it out with disgust.*]

BULSTRODE: 'Rainwear Society'?

GAVIN [*moving towards him*]: Ah. That, now. We do regard as terribly important!

BULSTRODE: The '*Rainwear* Society'?

GAVIN: They suffer such frightful loneliness. Unless they realize there are others exactly like them ...

BULSTRODE: *Who* suffers such terrible loneliness?

GAVIN: People who like rainwear.

BULSTRODE [*puzzled*]: Well, I like rainwear. I *quite* like rainwear. I mean, particularly when it's raining ...

GAVIN [*explaining patiently*]: My dear A ... My dear Curate. Your affection for rainwear, although genuine, I've no doubt, is detached. For people like us, you understand, macs have no sexual significance ...

BULSTRODE [*with rising astonishment*]: You mean you are using the Church, the House of God, for people to sit around and fall in love with their Burberrys?

GAVIN: Mr Bulstrode ...

BULSTRODE: *A. K.* Bulstrode ...

GAVIN: A. K. ... I have no idea what form your own particular brand of Christianity takes ...

BULSTRODE: Well, it certainly doesn't take the form of diving into Aquascutum's and saying a short prayer ...

GAVIN: I think the important thing, the *one* thing is tolerance towards sexual minorities ...

[MADGE *opens the door of the kitchen and goes into the hall.*]

BULSTRODE: Towards those who cherish their macs?

GAVIN: Not all of us can achieve normal satisfaction through the love of a good woman.

[MADGE *comes into the room. She crosses in silence. Finds a cigarette packet, takes one out and lights it. She straightens up wearily.*]

MADGE: I've done the tea things.

GAVIN [*genuinely enthusiastic*]: Well, congratulations, dear.

MADGE: I chucked it away. In the tidy bin! My head's splitting ... We need a thunderstorm.

BULSTRODE [*he moves to look out of the window*]: I don't suppose there's any reason why you shouldn't have one. With faith.

GAVIN [*tentatively*]: Madge ...

MADGE: Yes, Gavin?

GAVIN: You haven't disposed of all our crockery?

MADGE: Why not ...?

GAVIN: Well, you see ... I asked the Bishop to drop in for ... for a bite to eat on his way to Telly Centre ...

[*Long pause. Then* MADGE *looks at* GAVIN.]

MADGE [*with bitter intensity*]: You hate me, Gavin. Don't you? You've always hated me!

GAVIN: Now, my dear. Why should you say that ...?

MADGE: You want to make me look ridiculous! That's all. Just ridiculous! The Bishop here!

GAVIN: Why should that make you look ridiculous, Madge?

MADGE: Because there's absolutely nothing for him to eat!

GAVIN: Martin's a most tremendously modest person ...

MADGE: He can have his modesty for supper. That's all he'll get!

GAVIN: He's quite prepared to take pot luck.

MADGE: There's no pot luck ... No luck of any sort!

GAVIN: But there must have been something for our supper ...

MADGE: The slice of Mothers Pride and a frozen kipper for you. My head's splitting! Won't it ever rain? I couldn't take a bite of anything.

GAVIN: Surely there's an egg?

MADGE: Why surely? Why do you take it for granted there should be an egg? You expect too much of me. Am I meant to trail eggs around with me all the time? Just in case a bishop drops in unexpectedly?

BULSTRODE [*moving towards them*]: Look, no one wants to butt in. On any sort of domestic disagreement ...

GAVIN: Our new Curate. A. K. Bulstrode ...

MADGE [*turning away*]: Oh, I've met him! I suppose he'll need feeding too.

BULSTRODE: Sometimes a third party can lend a helping hand. It seems quite a simple problem.

MADGE: Of course it's simple. There's nothing to eat!

BULSTRODE: Well. Well now, Mrs Faber. Faced with a problem, as no one knows better than your husband, as no one has more experience than 'Sir' – there's one obvious person to apply to, isn't there, Rector?

GAVIN [*hopeful*]: You mean Mr Slocum? The wet fishmonger in Wainwright Avenue. Marvellous old character with a straw boater ...

BULSTRODE: Mr Slocum?

GAVIN: Plaice and chips. Absolutely *super*! Martin'd adore a nice bit of Mr Slocum's fish, Madge.

MADGE: He can have one frozen kipper – and you can sit round with hungry eyes and watch him eat it!

GAVIN: But Madge, Mr Slocum ...

MADGE: It's six o'clock! Mr Slocum's shut at five. Anyway, it's early closing.

BULSTRODE [*quietly*]: It wasn't to Slocum, the wet fish man, I suggested we might put in an application, sir.

GAVIN: You mean – fall back on Tesco's?

MADGE: Tesco's is shut. You hate me – that's the answer to it.

BULSTRODE: Not to Tesco's ...

GAVIN: Perhaps they're frying in Deptford Broadway ...

MADGE [*with mounting rage*]: You're torturing me, Gavin. They don't fry on Thursdays ...

BULSTRODE [*businesslike*]: You know quite well who we've got to apply to on this one, don't you, sir?

GAVIN: If you know better than my wife about the shops in this area.

BULSTRODE: Not in this area. There's a place that never closes. Even on Thursdays. Will you be taking prayers tonight, Rector?

MADGE [*laughs bitterly*]: Prayers! He won't be taking anything. Neither will the Bishop.

GAVIN: This isn't the Victorian age. We don't have family prayers here. Whatever are you thinking about?

MADGE: He wants to be a martyr. That's what he wants.

BULSTRODE: I was thinking about prayers.

GAVIN: We're just not that sort of people!

MADGE: You want to be a martyr. Don't you, Gavin. I know why you asked the Bishop. You want everyone to see you've got a wife that's perfectly useless. That's why. 'Look at her, Bishop. What a martyr I am. She can't mend a sock. She can't stitch the hem of a surplice. She's useless with the hassocks and there's no wet fish for supper. And as far as the bed department ...!'

GAVIN [*horrified*]: Madge!

[BULSTRODE *is standing in the middle of the room. He lifts his eyes to heaven.*]

BULSTRODE [*in a loud voice*]: Almighty and Most Merciful Father. Who helped us bring our bombs in dead on target in the late, great struggle ... and who watches over us in the dangerous days of so-called peace ... Look down we pray on these your servants who have got themselves in a bit of a fix this night, being Thursday night and local early closing.

Provide for them if it be Thy will O Lord . . . From the fullness
of thy great Supermarket of the Skies.

[*As he prays* GAVIN *is standing embarrassed, looking at the
ground.* MADGE *goes to the window*.]

GAVIN: What an extraordinary prayer! [*He goes and sits on the
sofa.*]

BULSTRODE [*his head bowed reverently*]: We also pray for His
Royal Highness the late Duke of Gloucester, Her Majesty the
Queen, the Queen Mother and all members of the Royal
family. We ask your blessing on all our forces overseas . . .

MADGE: My head! [*She opens the window.*]

BULSTRODE [*looks up again*]: And as for Mrs Faber's head. May
this close weather break up, O Lord. A heavy rainstorm would
be most refreshing at this particular time. In the name of the
Father, the Son and the Holy Spirit . . .

GAVIN [*rising*]: Yes. Well, I think we've had enough of that,
thank you, Curate.

BULSTRODE: Don't thank me, sir. It won't have anything to do
with me. I think I'll go up to my quarters. If you'll excuse me.
Church Parade certainly takes the spunk out of a person. [*He
goes out of the door. We see him standing quite still in the hall.*]

GAVIN: I hope he's not going to do that every evening. I do find
prayers enormously embarrassing.

[MADGE *puts her hand out of the window.* GAVIN *looks at his
watch.*]

GAVIN [*goes to the hi-fi. Takes off the Queen*]: Seven o'clock. I
promised to take this disc down to the organ loft. There's a
rehearsal. [*He's putting the record in its sleeve.*] Two really
super boys from Hebe's Hairstyles want their union blessed.
I thought Queen might be rather appropriate. While I'm down
there . . . I'll see if I can rustle up some eggs.

MADGE: Gavin, I distinctly felt a splodge of rain on my hand!

[*There's a sudden huge burst of thunder. Sound of rain pouring.*]

GAVIN [*disturbed*]: Well I'm sure it's pure fluke. Oh dear . . .

MADGE: My headache's going. I can feel it going . . .!

GAVIN: Pure chance, my dear. Pure fluke! [*He looks at the window, worried.*] Let us devoutly hope.

[*Black-out. In it we hear a clock striking. It goes on through the scene till it has struck eight.*]

SCENE TWO

As the light returns we see MADGE *in the living room. She is sitting on the sofa,* BULSTRODE *is standing in the hall. He opens the living-room door and goes in.*

BULSTRODE: Headache better is it, after the storm? It cleared the air.

MADGE: The air does get grubby round here occasionally.

BULSTRODE: It's so perfectly simple. One only has to put in an application. In the proper form naturally ...

MADGE: I enjoyed your prayers.

BULSTRODE: Yes. Good fun aren't they?

MADGE [*she finds herself a cigarette*]: Gavin hates prayers. We hardly ever get prayers at the Rectory.

BULSTRODE: Really? How do you cope with sin in that case?

MADGE: Sin? Gavin doesn't believe in sin either. People can do anything they like as far as he's concerned ...

BULSTRODE: And do they?

MADGE: What?

BULSTRODE: Do anything they like.

MADGE: Oh yes. It would surprise you sometimes. The type of people he's had round to see him! The mackintosh brigade! ... You don't approve of that, do you?

BULSTRODE: There's no doubt a line to be drawn. Even a simple mac can slide into sin, if we let it.

MADGE: Sin, yes! Such a good word. SIN! Gavin never uses it. I never imagined the Rectory like this ...

BULSTRODE: How ... how did you imagine it?

MADGE: I thought of visits from fallen girls ... They'd pour their heart out and we'd help them struggle against temptation. Or if it were too late ...

BULSTRODE: What then ...?

MADGE: Find them jobs perhaps. In Bourne and Hollingsworth's. Arrange the adoption of the baby. The last fallen girl we had here, Gavin lent her a book on Bondage – to enlarge her sexual repertoire ...

BULSTRODE: Look here! The devil's been having a high old time in St Barnabas Without, I can see. We've got to hit him for six, that gentleman!

MADGE [*contemptuous*]: It's all talk, of course. Gavin couldn't tie a knot to save his life!

BULSTRODE [*worried*]: He doesn't try, does he . . . ?

MADGE: I can't think so. He lends them the hall Thursday evenings. On Fridays the place is full of little bits of rope. Gavin says it comes in marvellously handy for the Scouts . . .

BULSTRODE: You mean he actually encourages it?

MADGE: You wouldn't do *that*, would you?

BULSTRODE: I should tell them the truth, quite frankly. You may be practising knots on Thursday, I'd say. But they'll be frying tomorrow . . . Deep frying!

MADGE: Oh dear! That reminds me . . . [*She moves to the door.*]

BULSTRODE: They're all on their way to one place! And the mackintosh members.

MADGE [*turning to him from the door*]: You don't mean . . .?

BULSTRODE: Hell, Mrs Faber. That's where *they'll* go. Give them enough rope.

MADGE [*nostalgic*]: Hell! Gavin hasn't spoken of that since we got married.

BULSTRODE: Perhaps you two have been getting into some sort of rut, Mrs Faber?

MADGE: Yes, perhaps . . . Hell! It seems so long since we even thought about it . . . I must try and find something for supper . . . [*She opens the door.*]

BULSTRODE: Seek and ye shall find, Mrs Faber.

[MADGE *goes into the kitchen. Starts looking hopelessly into one or two cupboards. There's a ring on the front door bell.*]

BULSTRODE: All right. I'll go.

[BULSTRODE *opens the front door. The* BISHOP *is standing there. He is a surprisingly young bishop, wearing a long mackintosh, buttoned at his neck, and a cap. He carries a briefcase.*]

BISHOP: Is the Rector in? I'm afraid I'm a little early . . . I'll go straight into the Holy of Holies . . .

BULSTRODE: The *what* ...?

BISHOP: Where he receives visitors. Down at the hall, is he? Of course, it's Thursday.

[*The* BISHOP *moves into the living room.* BULSTRODE *follows him, staring with distaste at the* BISHOP's *mackintosh as the* BISHOP *puts his briefcase on the table.*]

BULSTRODE: Aren't you going to take it off ...?

BISHOP [*takes off his cap, throws it on the sofa*]: I haven't seen the Rector for ages. I've been tied up such a lot recently ...

BULSTRODE [*horrified*]: You've been *what*?

BISHOP: We'll have lots and lots to talk about.

BULSTRODE [*pointing at the mac*]: Including *that* object, no doubt.

BISHOP: What object?

BULSTRODE: Your rainwear! Doesn't it ever occur to you to be ashamed? Making a fetish of a thing like that!

BISHOP: My dear man! This is a perfectly ordinary Burberry.

BULSTRODE: Probably only a part of your vast collection ...

[*In the kitchen* MADGE *sits down discouraged at the table.*]

BISHOP [*starting to undo his mac*]: Perhaps you'd like to take it?

BULSTRODE [*backing away*]: Believe me I want nothing whatsoever to do with it. It's your problem. You've just got to solve it yourself. No reason why you shouldn't, given guts!

BISHOP: My dear fellow. What *are* you talking about?

BULSTRODE: You! Mac-wearer!

BISHOP: But naturally. It's raining. Hadn't you noticed?

BULSTRODE: Oh, there's always an excuse for everything! Is there anything wrong with a little self-control? Anything whatever?

[MADGE *gets up and approaches the fridge with a sigh.*]

BISHOP: Look. Have you got some sort of obsession? With waterproofs?

[*In the kitchen* MADGE *pulls open the fridge door. She looks at it in amazement as a packet of peas, frozen chips and wrapped fish fall out on to the floor.*]

MADGE: Oh my God!

[*In the living room the* BISHOP *has taken off his mac revealing his purple stock, dog collar and pectoral cross.*]

BULSTRODE: My God!

BISHOP: Merely your Bishop.

BULSTRODE: The Supremo! Purple shirt front. Pectoral cross up. Look here. I'm afraid I've put up the most enormous black.

[*A key turns in the front door.* GAVIN *comes into the hall.* MADGE *calls from the kitchen.*]

MADGE: Gavin? Is that you, Gavin?

BULSTRODE: Look here. I'll hang it up for you.

[BULSTRODE *gathers up the* BISHOP's *cap and mac.* GAVIN *goes into the kitchen.* MADGE *is standing by the fridge, holding the door open.*]

MADGE: Just look at this!

GAVIN: What an unusual amount of fish!

MADGE: And frozen chips. And peas, Gavin ...

[BULSTRODE *comes out into the passage, hangs up the* BISHOP's *mac and stands listening to the voices from the kitchen.*]

GAVIN: What's that in the bread bin? [*He looks in the bread bin on top of the fridge.*]

MADGE: I hadn't noticed.

[GAVIN *opens the bread bin. It's full of bread.*]

GAVIN: Super loaves! I didn't know Mr Slocum did French bread.

MADGE: He doesn't!

GAVIN: But he *was* open, wasn't he?

MADGE: Of course he wasn't open. I told you. It's Thursday!

GAVIN: Then wherever ...?

MADGE: You *know*, Gavin. You really do *know*, don't you?

[BULSTRODE *goes quickly back into the living room, greets the* BISHOP.]

BULSTRODE: Bulstrode. A. K. Bulstrode. The new Curate. I hope I haven't caused too much embarrassment.

[*In the kitchen* GAVIN *is staring at the fridge and crossing himself.*]

MADGE: Oh Gavin! You haven't done that since we were courting.

[*Black-out.*]

[*Sound of Simon and Garfunkel singing on record. Lights go up. The* BISHOP *is comfortable, his legs up on the sofa, smoking a small cigar.* GAVIN *is in the armchair. They are listening to* SIMON AND GARFUNKEL *on the hi-fi.*]

BISHOP: Super, isn't it!

GAVIN: Absolutely super. What I say is you can't really beat Simon and Garfunkel.

BISHOP: Gavin.

GAVIN: Yes, Martin . . .

BISHOP: I suppose we ought to take this opportunity . . .

GAVIN: Well, yes!

BISHOP: Of seeing exactly where we've got on the Inter-denominational Gay Persons . . . [*He gets up, takes some papers out of his briefcase and goes to the table.*] I've got a bit of bumph here . . . would you care to glance?

[GAVIN *switches off the hi-fi and joins the* BISHOP *at the table.*]

GAVIN: Oh, love to, Martin. How super!

[*They sit together at the table.*]

BISHOP: You see, we've got Jewish and Roman Gays and Moslem Gays. You don't know any gay Hindus by any chance?

GAVIN: Well, I could ask around . . .

BISHOP: Super if you would.

GAVIN: Probably some on the buses. That might be a job for Bulstrode . . .

BISHOP: Well, I don't know about Bulstrode. He might not be quite the person.

GAVIN: You think not, Bish . . . Martin.

BISHOP: He does seem to have a blind unreasoning prejudice against *macs*, for instance . . . I mean, it'd be dreadful if he came up against a gay Hindu wearing a mackintosh . . .

> [*In the kitchen* BULSTRODE *is washing up with his shirt sleeves rolled up.* MADGE *is drying the plates dreamily. During the following scene the* BISHOP *and* GAVIN *work together in the living room, talking quietly.*
> *Light favours the kitchen.*]

BULSTRODE: Known the padre a long time, have you?

MADGE: Since I was eighteen. We joined the same Bible study group. I thought he was beautiful.

BULSTRODE: Well, it takes all sorts . . .

MADGE: I forced myself not to look at him.

BULSTRODE: I understand.

MADGE: I knew it would be wrong. Terribly wrong . . .

BULSTRODE: Aware of sin? Wisely.

MADGE: I prayed every night to be delivered from the temptation of Gavin Faber. I wanted some other girl to get him.

BULSTRODE: And did they?

MADGE: Apparently not. He was a virgin then and he is now, to the best of my knowledge, information and belief.

BULSTRODE [*handing her a plate*]: My dear Mrs Faber . . . however did that come about?

MADGE: I wanted him passionately. But I knew that even to speak to him would be a sin. I prayed to God I wouldn't be chosen to accompany him on the Deprived Children's Seaside Outing . . .

BULSTRODE: Your prayers were answered?

MADGE: They were denied! I was chosen . . . [*She is polishing the plates, on and on during this speech.*] There was a child there. A little pale girl. Well. None of them had ever seen the sea before – or heard it. She thought the waves advanced on her furiously, roaring like a lion. She ran from them in terror screaming. As I held her trembling in my arms I saw in her eyes such a fierce and fearless joy . . . it was exactly how I felt when I first saw the bulge in the front of Gavin's Jantzens!

[BULSTRODE *gently takes the plate from her and puts it down on the table.*]

MADGE: Thank you.

BULSTRODE: Mrs Faber. Why exactly are you telling me this?

MADGE: If I touched it I knew I was condemned to Hell fire. And yet I knew it was my destiny to touch it, sooner or later.

BULSTRODE: Later. I hope.

MADGE: The children lit a fire of driftwood and we sat round in a circle. Gavin led the community singing. 'Under the Spreading Chestnut Tree'. He touched his nipples. His forehead. He spread out his arms like branches. I watched him grow under the black wool of his Jantzens as he gazed at me. The wind blew a sandstorm against my bare legs and my teeth chattered with excitement ... I swore not to go near him, but on the charabanc home I pushed away the sour-smelling children with their wet towels and claimed a seat beside him! He had trousers on then. Pale grey flannel bags.

BULSTRODE: In the chara? Well, naturally.

MADGE: It would be a sin, I whispered to him, if I were to touch you there ...

BULSTRODE: What did 'Sir' say?

MADGE [*disgusted*]: He told me it wouldn't be a sin at all. That it was perfectly natural and God would understand ...

[*They go on washing up together.*]

BULSTRODE [*shocked*]: He should never have said that!

MADGE: He certainly shouldn't. From that moment I began to lose interest.

BULSTRODE: And ... the padre?

MADGE: Judging from the appearance of his fly buttons my sudden boredom communicated itself. 'Don't be frightened,' he said. 'There's no sort of sin about it. God doesn't care twopence about a little nooky, provided it's done with sincerity!'

BULSTRODE [*looking at her*]: But you didn't weaken ...?

MADGE: Well, if God wasn't going to take an interest – why should I?

BULSTRODE: You were bored?

MADGE: Utterly.

BULSTRODE: Sex. The physical side. Bored you, Mrs Faber?

MADGE: Once Gavin took the sin out of it for me ...

BULSTRODE: But you took a solemn vow of marriage to the Rector?

MADGE: With my body I thee worship! We were going to bed with each other on our wedding night. At least I could draw the attention of the Almighty to the fact.

BULSTRODE: And when you got there ...

MADGE: He stood in front of me. I remember it was a cold night. The gas fire was on in the bedroom. He brought me a warm drink. Cadbury's drinking chocolate. There was a ginger nut in the saucer, slightly softened by the spill as he carried it upstairs. Gavin was excited for some reason. His hand was far from steady. He had a great deal of trouble unknotting his pyjama cord. He'd tied a granny.

BULSTRODE: Mrs Faber. There are certain things one shouldn't know – about a brother cleric.

MADGE [*puzzled*]: That he ties grannies in his pyjama cord? He got it undone at last and they fell to his feet. Look at it, he said. Face it fearlessly. There is no sin here tonight. It was the effect of the drinking chocolate, I suppose. I fell asleep. Almost immediately. I'm not hopelessly wrong about sin, am I?

BULSTRODE: No, Mrs Faber. You're gloriously right! One hesitates to speak disrespectfully of a senior officer ... But it's my opinion 'Sir' gave you a totally wrong briefing on the subject of sin.

MADGE: I had hoped so.

BULSTRODE: He put you way off target. [*With disgust*] 'Nooky acceptable. If done with sincerity.' That's exactly how the Devil gets his propaganda out to the civilian population.

MADGE [*looks at him fascinated*]: The Devil?

BULSTRODE: When you hear that sort of nonsense talked. There's only one decent thing to do. Switch off the set!

MADGE: The Devil! One almost forgets about him. Living with Gavin.

BULSTRODE: Again one doesn't take issue with one's Wing-Co. But I might number your husband among the appeasers.

MADGE: The Devil was present. I know that. On the charabanc home from Herne Bay. I haven't seen much of him since.

BULSTRODE: Quite frankly, I can see our Rector ... flying out to meet the Prince of Darkness and coming back with a bit of paper and a rolled up brolly. [*He lets out the water, dries his hands on a towel*.]

MADGE: The Prince of Darkness ... It's awfully snobbish of course, but one does like a title.

BULSTRODE: You have to come down hard on sin if you're to send that Dark Gentleman packing ... That's the advice I used to give the rookies. Our AC plonks. At the first hint of a dirty thought ... Hop straight into a cold bath and say, 'Down Satan!' [*He moves close to* MADGE, *takes the last plate and drying up cloth from her*.]

MADGE [*staring at him, breathless*]: Down Satan! Sex ...

BULSTRODE: Please. There's a great deal too much talk about it.

MADGE: Gavin's not right. It is still a sin, isn't it? In your opinion?

BULSTRODE: Number one priority on the sin list. And that's not my opinion. That's official.

MADGE [*very quiet and breathlessly excited*]: Leading to Hell?

BULSTRODE: Straight downstairs. No question about it!

MADGE: Gavin told me they'd done away with Hell. He waited till after we'd married to tell me that ...

BULSTRODE: Done away with Hell? Don't you believe it.

MADGE [*moving away from him*]: Like slum clearance! They'd pull down Hell and build new towns with public washing machines and nothing to do in the evenings ...

BULSTRODE [*moving after her with the plate*]: If there isn't any Hell – what's the use of turning out for Church Parade? You can't have one without the other.

MADGE [*standing against the table*]: So there's a risk. Always a risk, Mr ...

BULSTRODE: Bulstrode. A. K. Bulstrode ...

MADGE [*looking at him*]: If one should engage in any sort of intimacy. Not being a married person.

[BULSTRODE *puts down the plate and stands very close to her*.]

MADGE: Even thinking about it.

BULSTRODE: Even that ... If I were to allow myself for an instant to turn my thoughts to you, Mrs Faber ...

MADGE: Downstairs?

BULSTRODE: Risking it. Most definitely.

MADGE: Risking it ...? And, of course, the slightest sort of a move – or gesture ...

BULSTRODE: Dicing, Mrs Faber. With death I'd say.

MADGE: So what would be the answer then? In the face of temptation ...

BULSTRODE: There is a cold bath available, I imagine – at almost any hour in the Rectory?

MADGE: Would you wish me to run one for you, Mr A. K. Bulstrode?

BULSTRODE: No. No, I'd rather not. I'd rather fight this thing on my own. We stood alone in the late great struggle, if you remember. Absolutely single-handed! I expect we'll win through in the end.

MADGE: Do you? Do you expect so?

BULSTRODE: One must simply take every care, that's all.

MADGE: What sort of precautions, Mr Bulstrode?

BULSTRODE: Not to be left alone. For instance while the Bishop and your husband are chatting it up in the snug. And if left alone ...

MADGE: If left alone?

BULSTRODE: Not to approach too closely ...

MADGE: Approaching too closely would be dangerous?

BULSTRODE: No doubt of it.

MADGE: And any form of touch?

BULSTRODE: Even if accidental. [*He puts down the plate on the table, touching her as he does so.*]

BULSTRODE: Brushing past whilst giving a hand with the washing up ...

MADGE [*touches his arm*]: Like that?

BULSTRODE: Anything like that, Mrs Faber.

MADGE: And one is in danger. Of a period of down under?

BULSTRODE: A long stretch, I'd say. If not the full infinity.

MADGE [*thankfully*]: Oh, thank you, Mr Bulstrode. You've brought the joy back to nooky.

[*She throws her arms round* BULSTRODE *and kisses him. Light fades on the kitchen and increases in the living room.*]

GAVIN: Bishop.

BISHOP: No, Gavin. I'm 'Martin'.

GAVIN: Yes, Bishop, of course. Martin ... Where do you stand on miracles?

BISHOP: I don't know. Where do you stand on miracles, Gavin?

[BULSTRODE *and* MADGE *leave the kitchen quietly. Switch off the kitchen light.*]

BISHOP: I ask you that because I don't in any way wish to seem to influence your way of thinking ...

GAVIN: Naturally not.

[BULSTRODE *and* MADGE *are going quietly across the hall and upstairs.*]

BISHOP: As your Bishop, Gavin. I must simply ask you to consult your own conscience.

GAVIN: On miracles?

BISHOP: Yes.

GAVIN: It's not a subject I've thought much about actually.

BISHOP [*stands up and paces*]: Well, when one approaches the subject of miracles one must face two distinct possibilities.

GAVIN: Yes.

BISHOP: The one is that they are historically, let us say, theologically possible ...

GAVIN: I suppose so.

BISHOP: And the other is that they are not. Doesn't that rather put the matter in a convenient nutshell?

GAVIN: I suppose it does.

BISHOP: It's up to you then, Gavin. Quite honestly which of those two alternatives do *you* go for?

GAVIN: You mean as a matter of personal conscience?

BISHOP: Of course. Without my influencing you, as your Bishop, in any way.

GAVIN: No, indeed. You want my opinion on miracles?

BISHOP: Gavin. That's what I'm trying to grope for.

GAVIN: Well, to be honest with you. As one must try to be in a matter of this sort ... To be entirely honest.

BISHOP: Please.

GAVIN: I take the view that miracles are a lot of absolute bloody nonsense!

BISHOP [*laughing*]: Walking on water!

GAVIN [*laughing*]: Withering the fig tree!

BISHOP: The raising of the dead.

GAVIN: Take up thy bed and walk!

BISHOP: Dear me, yes. They're not to be taken literally.

GAVIN: Pull the other one, as we say down the Rochester Row Lads' Club. It's got bells on it!

BISHOP: They've got a lot of good sound theological sense. Those delinquent lads ... Yes ...

[GAVIN, *relieved, goes to the hi-fi.*]

GAVIN: Should we have the other side now?

BISHOP: The other side of the argument?

GAVIN: Actually I meant ... the other side of Simon and Garfunkel.

BISHOP: Super music. [*Laughs*] Loaves and fishes!

[GAVIN *puts down the record.*]

GAVIN: Martin, why do you regard miracles as so bloody ridiculous? Is there no possibility that God's speaking to us ...?

BISHOP: If God wanted to speak to us, you don't honestly think He'd do it by handing out a lot of bread and fishes.

GAVIN: I don't suppose you noticed ... But *we* had fish for supper.

BISHOP: Super plaice. Did you get it from dear old Mr Slocum in Wainwright Avenue?

GAVIN: No. No, I'm afraid Mr Slocum was closed.

BISHOP: I suppose you'd like me to ask you where you got it?

GAVIN: Please, Martin.

BISHOP: Where did you get it from?

GAVIN: Out of the fridge ...

BISHOP: Gavin, I thought you wanted a serious theological discussion.

GAVIN: The fridge was absolutely bursting with fish, Martin, and frozen chips. Up to seven o'clock it had been empty ...

BISHOP: How *much* fish exactly?

GAVIN: Martin.

BISHOP: Yes, Gavin.

GAVIN: Would you care to have a look for yourself?

BISHOP: Is it absolutely necessary?

GAVIN: I wouldn't have asked you but as the person in command ... of any sort of manifestation ...

BISHOP: Don't call it a manifestation. As yet there's absolutely no reason to think of it as a manifestation.

[GAVIN *leads the way to the door. From somewhere upstairs we can hear* MADGE's *voice singing 'Under the Spreading Chestnut Tree'. It stops. They cross the hall, enter the kitchen and* GAVIN *switches on the light and opens the fridge.*]

BISHOP: Christ! What an extraordinary amount of fish!

GAVIN: Do you suppose?

BISHOP: Do I suppose what?

GAVIN: Do you suppose that there's some perfectly simple scientific explanation?

BISHOP: Such as what exactly ...?

GAVIN: Well. There might have been ... let's say ... a couple of fish left in the fridge. Perhaps ... What do you call the stuff? Eggs ... little grey eggs ...

BISHOP: Roe? Is that what you were groping for ...?

GAVIN: Roe. Thank you. And in a way. In some ... quite simple scientific way. It's been so hot lately. Due to the rise in temperature ...

BISHOP: A rise of temperature in the fridge!

GAVIN: Well, as I say, I'm absolutely no marine biologist.

BISHOP: You certainly are not. That's becoming painfully obvious!

GAVIN: There might have been some transference of the vital seed.

BISHOP: Fecundatio ab extra!

GAVIN: You're so much more widely read than I am, Martin.

BISHOP: Between a couple of dead fish ... [*He slams the door of the fridge shut.*] It's a bloody good thing the Church of England exists for your sake, Gavin. I scarcely think you'd have shone in any other profession ...

GAVIN: Could we possibly ring up the Zoo? They must have some sort of information service.

BISHOP: That's what's wrong with the clergy today. You've become so helplessly dependent on the Zoo! [*He sits down at the kitchen table with a sigh.*] Just go through the events which led to this ludicrous happening, will you?

GAVIN [*trying hard to remember*]: You telephoned me ...

BISHOP: There was as I remember an incredible noise in the background.

GAVIN: It was the Queen.

BISHOP: Gavin ... Is it time you took a long rest from pastoral work?

GAVIN: You know, Martin. Fabulous group. Satin hot-pants. Eye make-up. Freddie Mercury ...

BISHOP: Just try to give me a lucid account ... This may be important ...

GAVIN: I asked you to dinner. Well, by some miracle you happened to be free.

BISHOP: By some chance. We won't use that word unless it's forced upon us!

GAVIN: By some chance. You were free ... So I told Madge you were going to do us the honour. I said there'd be four ... counting the Curate ... It was then I learnt she'd thrown the washing up in the tidy bin.

BISHOP: Does she often do that?

GAVIN: It's her nerves. These big old rectories are a strain on the wife's temper. Also it was unbearably hot ...

BISHOP: Yes?

GAVIN: Stifling! Madge gets her headaches when it's close.

BISHOP: So far as I remember it was raining cats and dogs. I had to grab a Burberry before coming on to you ...

GAVIN: Yes. The weather broke. There was a storm. That relieved Madge's headache and ... Well, I remember. We were praying for a thunderstorm ...

BISHOP [*rises, perturbed*]: You were *praying*?

GAVIN: Well, not me, Bishop. Not me, Martin! Oh, certainly not. That would have been pure God-bothering, wouldn't it? Prayer for me, of course, is a moment of getting in touch with

Professor Jung's collective unconscious and all those who move with the spirit of the Universe . . .

BISHOP [*sarcastic*]: 'Hallo Jung lovers wherever you are . . .'

GAVIN [*laughing politely*]: Super *joke*! No. It wasn't me praying. Not at all. It was the new fellow. The Curate.

BISHOP: Who?

GAVIN: A. K. Bulstrode.

BISHOP: What did he do?

GAVIN: He prayed for rain.

BISHOP: And what happened?

GAVIN: It rained . . . [*He waves his hand nervously.*]

BISHOP [*irritated*]: Do try and control yourself! Gavin . . .

GAVIN: I am.

BISHOP: I thought I detected your left hand . . . Itching to trace a cruciform shape.

GAVIN [*putting his hand away*]: Oh, no, Bish . . . No, Martin. Not me. Certainly!

BISHOP [*pacing the kitchen*]: I would like to come, if you can be very calm about this, to the subject of the fish.

GAVIN: Yes. Of course, the fish . . . [*He sits down, weak.*] Well, when I told Madge you were coming to dinner . . .

BISHOP: Yes. When you told her. How did she react?

GAVIN: She burst – into uncontrollable tears.

BISHOP: Is that the effect of all my visitations on the wives of the Senior Clergy?

GAVIN: It was a question of provisions. As A. K. Bulstrode would call it!

BISHOP: Him again?

GAVIN: The cupboard was bare. Or rather the fridge was. At least, there was nothing but a kipper and a slice of Mothers Pride.

BISHOP: Dear me. The Church today does exist on a shoestring! You should have really come to the Palace . . . Peter and I can always knock up a simple piperade. Are you telling me, Gavin, that at seven p.m. this evening your fridge was empty . . .!

GAVIN: It was A. K. Bulstrode who said it.

BISHOP: What?

GAVIN: That there was one obvious person to apply to.

BISHOP: He wasn't referring, then, to your fishmonger Slocum?

GAVIN: I'm afraid it was to the Almighty.

BISHOP: I'm afraid so too. What happened then?

GAVIN: Bulstrode ...

BISHOP: A. K. Bulstrode?

GAVIN: Exactly! Said a short prayer and went up to have a look at his quarters.

BISHOP: He seems to be exercising a powerful military influence on all of you.

GAVIN: Later Madge took a last look in the fridge.

BISHOP: What was the result ...?

GAVIN: An ... an extraordinary superfluity of plaice.

BISHOP: Plenty of bread too, if I remember.

GAVIN [*gloomy*]: Those crunchy French loaves that Madge seems to find ...

BISHOP: Well, it's obvious, isn't it?

GAVIN: Is it?

BISHOP: Gavin. I know your mind is full of *Honest to God* and Bonhoeffer and Teilhard de Chardin. But if you cast your mind back to that bulky black book we were made to read in Theological College ...

GAVIN: The one with the *ghastly* illustrations?

BISHOP: You will surely, recognize a certain Biblical parallel.

GAVIN: I've recognized it already. You do mean loaves and fishes, don't you, Martin?

BISHOP: Your quickness astounds me!

GAVIN: Then it is a m—

BISHOP [*holding up a hand to interrupt him*]: First we must reflect on all other explanations. I pass over your suggestion of the virgin conception of a dried kipper in the fridge. Question. Is the phenomenon one which can be explained by the psycho-somatic nature of the disease? Answer. This is not a pheno-menon of healing, it is a phenomenon of fish. Question. Can it be explained by the delusions of witnesses? Answer. I do not suffer from delusions. I separated the real fish from genuine fishbone. I broke the crusty bread and spread butter on it. I recollect the taste perfectly distinctly. Conclusion. We are driven to the conclusion that this is a Cosmic Miracle ...

GAVIN [*gloomy*]: I thought you might be driven there in the end.

BISHOP: Brought down upon us by none other than the person of your new Curate, for whom I am bound as your Bishop to hold you directly responsible.

GAVIN: A. K. Bulstrode?

BISHOP: We had none of this trouble in the Diocese before you brought him on the scene.

GAVIN: Martin.

BISHOP: I think it better now that you address me as Bishop. In the usual way.

GAVIN [*apologetic*]: I'm dreadfully sorry, Bishop ... I didn't actually select ...

BISHOP: You put in for a curate. Rector, do you realize what this means ...?

GAVIN: I suppose it's the sort of thing they might get their teeth into – on 'Nationwide'.

BISHOP: It doesn't matter about you, Rector. You emerge from total obscurity and any touch of the limelight, however lurid, will no doubt be welcome to you. But I appear on 'Any Questions'. I debate on the 'Epilogue'. I have undertaken to make our beliefs acceptable to the average man of reasonable good will and scientific enlightenment. I have reliably informed him that God is no longer *up there*, Rector. And not *out there*, either, delivering us surprise gifts like a sort of transcendental fishmonger! God is within you! Deep, down, *inside you*. At first sight I must admit it seems an odd sort of place to put him.

GAVIN: I do realize we've caused a bit of a muck-up here in this Parish ...

BISHOP: Muck-up! What do you want to achieve, Rector? A return to the days of darkness and superstition ... Do you want to be ridiculed in the *Guardian* and denounced in *New Society*. With queues on crutches all the way down Deptford Broadway and stalls erected for the sale of plastic statuettes of A. K. Bulstrode? The prospect's too horrible to contemplate.

GAVIN: Couldn't we perhaps unfrock the fellow?

BISHOP: Oh yes. We could also burn him at the stake. And I could conduct a service of exorcism with Bell, Book and Candle all round your fridge. Our aim, Rector, is to keep miracles out of the Sunday papers.

[BULSTRODE *and* MADGE *come hand in hand down the stairs into the living room.* MADGE *is smiling as she puts a record on the hi-fi.*]

BISHOP: That is entirely up to you ... He's your Curate. Look after him.

GAVIN: But how?

BISHOP: Exercise a little clerical discipline, Rector. Keep a firm hand on his tiller.

GAVIN: I'll do my best, Bishop. I'll watch him ...

BISHOP: Like a hawk.

GAVIN: I promise you. He won't get up to his tricks again in *this* house. You can trust me, Bishop.

BISHOP: I hope I can. I only hope I can ... We don't want another breath of a miracle from that particular gentleman!

[*The hi-fi is playing 'Bridge Over Troubled Water'.* BUL-STRODE *and* MADGE *are dancing together, doing a rather deft fox-trot as the lights fade to black-out.*]

[*In the black-out 'Bridge Over Troubled Water' gives way to 'Amazing Grace'.*
As the light comes up GAVIN *is on his knees in the living room praying. In the kitchen* BULSTRODE *is cutting sandwiches which he wraps and puts in his pocket.* MADGE *is just going out of the front door. She opens it to reveal* MR SLOCUM, *the fishmonger, in a straw hat and striped apron. He has a bill in his hand. She points to the living room and* MR SLOCUM *goes in to interrupt* GAVIN's *prayers.*]

MR SLOCUM: I'm surprised at you ...

GAVIN: Why? Isn't this a pretty conventional position. For a vicar?

MR SLOCUM: I'm surprised how you can go on your knees to Almighty God – with your bills unpaid for exactly four months.

[GAVIN *gets to his feet, switches off the hi-fi.*]

GAVIN: Why, it's Mr Slocum. Dear old Mr Slocum. How is the wet fish business exactly?

MR SLOCUM: How do you expect it to be – with no one meeting

their obligations! As if we hadn't got enough to put up with – package cod in Tesco's, fish fingers . . . frozen clam chowder and all that convenience nonsense! And who can you find today to stand with their fingers in cold water scaling a turbot . . . Who can you?

GAVIN [*puzzled*]: I don't know. Very few people, I imagine.

MR SLOCUM: Would you do it? Come on, Vicar. Would you get your hands in icy water on a freezing winter's day and lug the private parts out of skate, would you?

GAVIN: Not if there was any sort of an alternative.

MR SLOCUM: Added to which there's unpaid bills to contend with.

GAVIN: I'm sure yours is a most troublesome profession.

MR SLOCUM: Attempts to run away from their liabilities by gentlemen of the Cloth.

GAVIN: Oh, come now, Mr Slocum. There may have been an oversight about some small amount . . .

MR SLOCUM: Small amount. Did you say *small* amount?

[*He hands the bill to* GAVIN *who reads it.*]

GAVIN: 'July 2nd. To supply of wet fish and frozen veg. to the Rectory.'

MR SLOCUM: Four months ago! Four months. That bill has been ignored.

GAVIN: Fourteen pounds and seven p! For one evening!

MR SLOCUM: The wife and I thought you must be having a bit of a fry up!

GAVIN [*puts the bill on the table*]: This is absurd. Oh, my God! Bulstrode!

[BULSTRODE *puts the packet of sandwiches in his pocket, leaves the kitchen and goes upstairs.*]

MR SLOCUM: And when I obliged you, sir. Closed up, we was. Sat down in front of 'Crossroads' with a beautiful bit of halibut. And your boy came knocking at the door . . .

GAVIN: My . . . my boy?

MR SLOCUM: Your filleter, sir. Your gaffer. Old fellow with a loud voice and a bit of a haddock's eye to him . . .

GAVIN: A remarkably good description.

MR SLOCUM: 'Please, for God's sake. In the name of the Lord ...' That's how he expressed himself. 'They're in sudden desperate need of fish up at the Rectory.'

GAVIN [*greatly distressed*]: Blind! I have been blind about this. The Bishop can't escape some responsibility ...

MR SLOCUM: I've been sending my bill. Regular.

GAVIN: I have little doubt that it was intercepted.

MR SLOCUM: Intercepted, was it?

GAVIN: Mr Slocum. You've been treated shabbily. And so have I. Very shabbily. You shall be paid! I assure you, you shall be paid. As soon as Mrs Faber gets back with the cheque book. She always carries my cheque book. For some reason she's more into cheque books than I am. I'm sorry you had to come here. It must have been embarrassing for you. Dreadfully embarrassing.

MR SLOCUM: Well, one doesn't like to push one's way into a person's prayers ... But when he's had the fish four months ...

GAVIN: I understand, Mr Slocum. I do understand. You are a most *super* wet fish man. One of the Old Brigade. We couldn't live without you. Now, if we just leave your bill here ... Mrs Faber has had to slip round to Doctor Piercey's, but the instant she gets back ...

MR SLOCUM [*moving to the door*]: Well, thank you, Reverend. Thank you very much.

GAVIN: Thank *you*, Mr Slocum. You have cleared up a great mystery!

[GAVIN *goes back to the table as* MR SLOCUM *lets himself out of the front door.* GAVIN *is staring hopelessly at the bill as* BULSTRODE *comes down the stairs with his kit bag packed and leans it against the wall. He is trying to open the front door quietly when* GAVIN *hears him.*]

GAVIN: Is that you, Bulstrode?

[*He opens the living-room door just as* BULSTRODE *is trying to escape.*]

BULSTRODE: Wing-Co.!

GAVIN: I want to see you, Bulstrode. [*He leads him back into the living room.*] Slocum was here!

BULSTRODE: Really? Who is Slocum?

GAVIN: The fishmonger.

BULSTRODE: What, are you planning another little 'do' for the Bishop?

GAVIN: And I have to tell you, Bulstrode, he cast considerable doubt on that miracle of yours.

BULSTRODE [*frowning*]: I don't know Slocum. Does he come to Church?

GAVIN: He's a perfectly ordinary, decent citizen ... of course he doesn't come to Church.

BULSTRODE [*laughing unexpectedly*]: You mean, he's not knotted up in any way? Oh, forgive me, sir, but you do lend yourself to it!

GAVIN [*primly*]: I mean, he's a perfectly rational man.

BULSTRODE [*serious*]: And he casts doubts on a miracle?

GAVIN: The Miraculous Appearance of the Fish in the Fridge.

BULSTRODE: Well ... rational men'll cast doubt on everything.

GAVIN: And he's got a bill to prove it!

[*He hands the bill to* BULSTRODE.]

BULSTRODE: That's ridiculous!

GAVIN: Your miracle.

BULSTRODE: I mean. The price!

GAVIN: I was deceived by you, Bulstrode! I was taken in! This just isn't a world where miracles happen ...

BULSTRODE: In a world where you have to pay this for plaice and frozen peas just about anything could happen. Excuse me, sir. Are you saying you don't believe in miracles?

GAVIN: I'll tell you what I believe! I believe you slunk out of here, Bulstrode. I believe you knocked up dear old Mr Slocum and dragged him away from 'Crossroads'. I believe you told him there was a fry-up at the Rectory and fish was urgently needed. I believe you crept back and filled our fridge with a ridiculous amount of provender, and I believe you have been shamelessly nicking old Mr Slocum's bills from the hall table.

[*Pause.* BULSTRODE *looks at him.*]

BULSTRODE: It seems a remarkably boring explanation.

GAVIN: It's what I choose to believe . . .

BULSTRODE: Well, if you choose to believe a boring explanation, all I can say, sir, is your life will be singularly dull.

GAVIN: If it's dull, it's better than being tricked!

BULSTRODE: Tricked? Who tricked you?

GAVIN: You did, Bulstrode.

BULSTRODE: How did I trick you?

GAVIN: And you tricked the Bishop. That good man Martin Spottiswoode. All that talk of miracles.

BULSTRODE: All *what* talk? I never mentioned miracles . . .

GAVIN: Didn't you? Perhaps you didn't. But you let us think . . .

BULSTRODE: I said a prayer. Later there was fish in the fridge. I left you to draw your own conclusions. From what I remember you telling me, it was you and the Bishop who brought up the subject of mir.......

GAVIN: You didn't disillusion us . . .

BULSTRODE: Who was I . . . to betray that faith which made you both so happy?

GAVIN: Happy? Martin Spottiswoode and I were both profoundly disturbed.

BULSTRODE: Not a bad thing! You've been saying your prayers ever since, I notice . . .

GAVIN: What use is prayer? On a basis of error?

BULSTRODE: Look here. How do you know it's error? That fridge was filled up . . . at a speed some highly intelligent people would call supernatural.

GAVIN: But Mr Slocum's evidence . . . !

BULSTRODE: Are you going to overturn a great system of theology on the evidence of one elderly agnostic fishmonger — whose herrings are none too fresh, if you want my opinion?

GAVIN: You can't worm your way out of this one, Bulstrode. Miracles simply don't happen. No one can defy the physical laws of the Universe.

[MADGE *is letting herself in at the front door*.]

BULSTRODE: Can't they honestly, sir? Don't despair. A fellow can have a damn good bash at it.

[MADGE *comes into the room. Very excited*.]

MADGE: Gavin. Oh, Gavin . . .!

GAVIN: Madge. What has come over you?

MADGE: I've got news . . .

GAVIN: Yes, so have I!

MADGE: Wonderful news!

GAVIN: Well, this isn't so wonderful . . .

MADGE: From Doctor Piercey.

GAVIN: From Slocum the fishmonger.

MADGE: He met me in the street. I didn't even have to go and wait in the surgery. The test's positive . . .

GAVIN: What test is that, Madge?

MADGE: The tests I've been having. I didn't tell you, Gavin. I didn't want to raise your hopes . . .

GAVIN: What hopes?

MADGE: Think of all we can do together. On days out. We'll take him to the seaside.

GAVIN: Take who, exactly?

MADGE: Oh, Gavin. I'm expecting . . .

GAVIN: Expecting what?

MADGE: Your son!

GAVIN: My son. What son? Madge. I don't know if you remember. Perhaps you don't recall. But it's hardly very likely . . .

MADGE: All the same, it's happened!

BULSTRODE: Put your arms round her, sir. Where are the physical laws of the Universe now?

[BULSTRODE *smiles at them and goes out of the room.* GAVIN *has his arm round* MADGE.]

GAVIN: Bulstrode! Madge. What an extraordinary person. What do you think of him, Madge? Do you think some people . . . have extraordinary powers. For Good?

MADGE: Think of him? Think of Mr Bulstrode? I think he's a gentleman.

[BULSTRODE *has picked up his kit bag and is going out of the front door.*]

Curtain.

MORE ABOUT PENGUINS, PELICANS
AND PUFFINS

For further information about books available from Penguins please write to Dept EP, Penguin Books Ltd, Harmondsworth, Middlesex UB7 0DA.

In the U.S.A.: For a complete list of books available from Penguins in the United States write to Dept DG, Penguin Books, 299 Murray Hill Parkway, East Rutherford, New Jersey 07073.

In Canada: For a complete list of books available from Penguins in Canada write to Penguin Books Canada Ltd, 2801 John Street, Markham, Ontario L3R 1B4.

In Australia: For a complete list of books available from Penguins in Australia write to the Marketing Department, Penguin Books Australia Ltd, P.O. Box 257, Ringwood, Victoria 3134.

In New Zealand: For a complete list of books available from Penguins in New Zealand write to the Marketing Department, Penguin Books (N.Z.) Ltd, P.O. Box 4019, Auckland 10.

In India: For a complete list of books available from Penguins in India write to Penguin Overseas Ltd, 706 Eros Apartments, 56 Nehru Place, New Delhi 110019.